CHRIST IN US

THE WORK OF THE HOLY SPIRIT IN MAN

BY ANDREW MURRAY

Originally Published as

THE SPIRIT OF CHRIST

Revised and Rewritten

BY GARY W. FREY

DEDICATION

This edited and revised work of Andrew Murray is dedicated to God the Father, who gave us God the Son, the Lord Jesus Christ, who gave us the Holy Spirit, who is the Spirit of Christ. This updated work is also dedicated to the memory of Andrew Murray, who sought after the Holy Spirit, who is the Spirit of Wisdom and Revelation, the Spirit of Christ in us. Mr. Murray presented this holy work to the world so very many years ago at the leading and through the revelation of the Spirit. We honor him and our God who inspired him to write it.

I also want to acknowledge our good friends Michael Van Vlyman, my publisher; Barbie Hanes for her stellar work in editing, and Paul Williams for his editing and encouragement. Thank you all for your faith in the project of this revised edition. We are in your debt.

And finally, I want to honor the memory of a precious saint, Aileen Bowers, who first introduced me to the original work, The Spirit of Christ, so many years ago. As she was led by the Holy Spirit, God used her to powerfully impact my life.

INTRODUCTION

I was first introduced to the original version of this book, originally published as The Spirit of Christ, by Andrew Murray, in 1988, one hundred years after its initial publication. At the time I was a young pastor of a very small, failing church, very full of myself, convinced that I knew God, and that everyone else needed to hear me and all of the great wisdom that I had. One day a dear older saint, a woman who had been part of my church for a couple of years, asked me to come over to her house; in reality it was more of a summons. She proceeded to confront me in love about my arrogance and pride, and my lack of Christ-like character, and that the failure of our church and my ministry was directly due to my own lack of knowledge of the Lord Jesus Christ. She went on to say something to the effect, "I don't doubt that there is a call of God on your life, Gary, but you are too full of yourself to allow a place for him to live out his life in you." She then handed me a copy of The Spirit of Christ. Her final words to me were, "Please read this. I am praying for you." Of course I denied her allegations, but in that deep place in my inner man I knew she was right, and that everything she confronted me with was true.

It wasn't long after that I began a downward spiral that led me into a long season of deep darkness, and ultimately questions about my faith in God, his call on my life, and even my entire reason for existence. It wasn't until years later as the Lord graciously began to restore me that I began to read The Spirit of Christ. At that time I was led to read a chapter every day for over a year. I read through the book at least a dozen times, and as I read Murray's words and insights day after day the Holy Spirit began to open me up to the great possibilities of life in Jesus Christ.

Today I would say that the dear saint's prayers have been answered, and that this book, The Spirit of Christ has been a powerful tool used by the Holy Spirit himself to help shape and transform me into a closer reflection of the life of Christ in me. He is not finished - there is still more.

This is not an easy book to read and understand. It was originally written in Dutch - Andrew Murray was a South African - and then translated into nineteenth century English, which can be very difficult for a twenty-first century reader to understand. In this updated and revised version, we have edited some of the words and sentences in order to provide a more concise flow and thought. In the original English edition there were words and sentence structures that are no longer in use today in our modern forms of English; these have been substituted with more relevant words and sentence structures, hopefully without changing the original meaning or context. Where possible we have tried to use alternatives to the male-only pronouns, which were predominant in the nineteenth century. However in those chapters and places where that could not be achieved, please understand that Murray, and we, are referring to all believers, both male and female.

Andrew Murray's revelation of the Holy Spirit as the Spirit of Christ, Christ in us, is not something we will comprehend merely through reading this book. Even in this revised version, some of his words may need to be read and reread, and prayed through numerous times. I have worked on this revised edition for over a year now, and I find myself in awe of the depths of the riches of the wisdom and knowledge of God presented in this book. I've read the original book dozens of times, but at times as I was rewriting, it was as if I was seeing something for the first time. At times as I was working on this manuscript the very presence of the Holy Spirit would settle on me. At other times I was deeply convicted at how my own life was still not fully living out what I was writing. But I realized that being conformed to the image of Christ is a life long process. Nevertheless, the writing of this revised book has been life changing for me.

This book is a Christian classic that needs to be in the hands of seeking believers today. It is as relevant today as it was in 1888, perhaps even more so; the Church of Jesus Christ is still in need of all that it teaches. It will provoke and challenge each of us to draw closer to God, and become familiar with the Holy Spirit that he has promised to deposit in us. That Spirit, who is the Spirit of Christ in us, will change us and transform us into the very image, likeness and nature of Christ himself, and from there we will manifest and reflect his life to a world that is shrouded in darkness.

If you are a devout follower of Andrew Murray and his original style of writing and sentence structure, you may not find this edition appealing. However, you may know precious saints who can relate to this updated version more so than the classic.

And for those who are not as familiar to him or his writings, hopefully, you will find this book to be a great blessing. May God richly bless you as you journey into The Spirit of Christ - Christ in us, the work of the Holy Spirit in man.

Gary Frey
Publisher and Editor
August 28, 2020

PREFACE

In times past believers met God, knew him, walked with him, and had the clear and full consciousness that they were dealing with the God of heaven, and through faith, the assurance that they and their lives were well pleasing to him. When the Son of God came to earth and revealed the Father, it was so that fellowship with God and the assurance of his favor might become clearer, and be the abiding portion of every child of God. When he was exalted to the throne of glory, it was that he might send down into our hearts the Holy Spirit, in which the Father and the Son have their own blessed life in heaven; and to maintain in us his divine power, the blessed life of fellowship with God. It was to be one of the marks of the New Covenant that each member of it should walk in personal communion with God. *'They shall teach no more every man his neighbor, know the Lord, for they shall all know Me, from the least to the greatest of them', says the Lord, 'For I will forgive their iniquity!'* (Jeremiah 31:34) The personal fellowship and knowledge of God in the Holy Spirit was to be the fruit of the pardon of sin. The Spirit of God's own Son, sent into our hearts to do a work as divine as the work of the Son in redeeming us; to displace our life and replace it by the life of Christ in power, to make the Son of God divinely and consciously present with us always - this was what the Father had promised as the distinctive blessing of the New Testament. The fellowship of God as the three-in-one was now to be within us; the Spirit revealing the Son in us, and through him the Father.

No one will deny that there are very few believers today who experienced this walk with God, this life in God, such as their

Father has prepared for them. Nor can we admit or dispute what the cause of this failure is. It is acknowledged on all hands that the Holy Spirit, through whose divine omnipotence, this inner revelation of the Son and the Father in the life and the likeness of the believer is to take place, is not known or acknowledged in the church as he should be. In our preaching and in our practice, he does not hold that place of prominence which he has in God's place and in his promises. While our creed on the Holy Spirit is orthodox and scriptural, his presence and power in the life of believers, in the ministry of the work, in the witness of the Church to the world, is not what the word promises or God's plan requires.

There are many who are conscious of this great need, and earnestly ask to know God's mind concerning it, and the way of deliverance out of it. Some feel that their own life is not what it should and might be. Many of them can look back to some special season of spiritual revival, when their whole life was apparently lifted to a higher level. The experience of the joy and the strength of the Savior's presence, as they learned that he would keep them trusting, was, for a time, very real and blessed. But it did not last - there was a very gradual decline to a lower level, with much vain effort and sad failure. They would long to know where the evil lies. There can be little doubt that the answer must be this: they did not know or honor the indwelling Spirit as the strength of their life, as the power of their faith, to keep them always looking to Jesus and to trusting in him. They did not know what it was to day by day wait in lowly reverence for the Holy Spirit to deliver them from the power of the flesh, and to maintain the wonderful presence of the Father and the Son within them.

There are many more, countless numbers of God's dear children, who as yet know little of any, even temporary experiences of a brighter life than one of never-ending stumbling and rising. They have lived outside of revivals and conferences; the teaching they receive is not especially helpful in the matter of entire consecration. Their surroundings are not favorable to the growth of the spiritual life. There may be moments of sincere longing to live more according to the will of God, but the prospect of its being really possible to walk and please God day by day, has hardly dawned upon them. They are strangers to the best part of their birthright as God's children, to the most precious gift of the Father's love in Christ, the gift of the Holy Spirit, to dwell in them, and to lead them.

I would greatly count it an unspeakable privilege if God would use me to bring these, his beloved children, the question of the Word, *Know you not that your body is the temple of the Holy Spirit which is in you?* and then tell them the blessed news of what the glorious work is, which the Spirit, whom they have with them, is able to do in each of them. If I might, I would show them what it is that has so hindered the Spirit from doing his blessed work. And I would explain how divinely simple the path is by which each upright soul can enter into the joy of the full revelation of the presence of the indwelling Jesus. I have humbly asked God that he would give, even in my feeble words, the quickening of his Holy Spirit, that through them, the thoughts, the truth, the life and the power of God may enter and shine into the hearts of many of his children, to bring in blessed reality and experience the wondrous gift of love of which they proclaim, the Life and the Joy of the Holy Spirit as he brings close and glorifies with them that Jesus, whom until now they have only known from a distance, high above them.

I must confess to still another wish. I have strong fears, (and I say this in deep humility), that in the theology of our churches the teaching and leading of the Spirit of truth, the anointing which alone teaches all things, does not have the practical recognition which a Holy God demands, and which our Savior meant him to have. In everything that concerns the Word of God and the Church of Jesus Christ, and the work of saving love to be done on the earth in the name of Christ, it was meant that the Holy Spirit should have the same and supreme place of honor that he had in the Church of the Acts of the Apostles. If the religious leaders of our day, the teachers, pastors, bible scholars and church councils, if our professors of theology and our commentators, and if our ministers and students, and writers and workers were all fully conscious of this fact, then surely the signs of that honor given and accepted, the marks of his holy presence would be clearer and his mighty works would be more manifest. I trust it has not been presumptuous of me to hope that what has been written may help remind us all that the first and the indispensable requirement for what is really to bear fruit for eternity, is that it be full of the power of the eternal Spirit.

I am well aware that it may be expected by men of intellect and culture, and also by our scientific theologians, that these words should bear the marks of scholarship, of force and thought, and power of expression. To these points I cannot dare to lay a claim to. Yet I venture to ask any of these honored brothers who may venture to read this book, to regard it at least as the echo of a cry for light rising from countless hearts, and as the stating of questions for the solution of which many are longing. There is a deep feeling throughout the Church, that Christ's own promise of what the Church should be, and its present state, do not correspond.

Of all questions in theology there is none that leads us more deeply into the glory of God, or that is of more intense, vital and practical importance for daily life, than that which deals with what is the consummation and culmination of the revelation of God and the work of redemption. Or in what way and to what extent God's Holy Spirit can dwell in, fill up, and make into a holy and beautiful temple of God, the heart of his child, with Christ reigning there, as an ever-present and almighty Savior. It is the question in theology of which the solution, if it were sought and found in the presence and teaching of the Spirit himself, would transform all our theology into that knowledge of God, which is eternal life.

We have no lack of theology, in every possible shape and form. But it is as if with all of our writing and preaching and working, that there is still something lacking. Is it not the power from on high the one thing we lack? May it not be that with all our love for Christ and labor for his cause, that we have not made the chief object of our desire what was the chief object of his heart when he ascended the throne, to have his disciples as a company of saints waiting to be clothed with the power of the Holy Spirit, that in that power of his manifested presence of their Lord, they might testify of him? May God raise from among our theologians many who shall give their lives to secure for God's Holy Spirit his recognition in the lives of believers, in the ministry of the word by tongue and pen, in all the work done in His Church.

I have noticed with deep interest, a renewed call to union in prayer, that Christian life and teaching may be increasingly subject to the Holy Spirit. I believe that one of the first blessings of this united prayer will be to direct attention to the reason why such prayer is not more evidently answered, and to the true preparation for receiving abundant answers. In my reading in connection with this subject, in my observation of the lives of believers, and in my personal experience, I have been very deeply impressed with one thought - it is that our prayer for the mighty working of the Holy Spirit through us and around us, can only be powerfully answered as *his indwelling* in every believer is more clearly acknowledged and lived out. We have the Holy Spirit within us; only he who is faithful in the lesser will receive the greater. As we first yield ourselves to be led by the Spirit, to confess his presence in us, as believers rise to realize and accept his guidelines in all their daily life, will our God be willing to entrust to us larger measures of his mighty workings. If we surrender ourselves entirely into his power, as our life ruling within us, he will give himself to us and take a more complete possession, and then work through us.

If there is one thing I desire, it is that the Lord may use what I have written, to make clear and impress this one truth: *it is as an Indwelling Life that the Holy Spirit must be known.* In a living, adoring faith, the indwelling Spirit must be accepted and treasured, until it becomes part of the consciousness of the new man - The Holy Spirit possesses me. In this faith the whole life, even the least of things, must be surrendered to his leading, while all that is of the flesh or self is crucified and put to death. If in this faith we wait on God for his divine leading and working, placing ourselves entirely at his disposal, then our prayer cannot remain unheard. There will be operations and manifestations of the Spirit's power in the Church and the world such as we could not dare to hope. The Holy Spirit only demands vessels entirely set apart to him. He will delight to manifest the glory of Christ our Lord.

I commit each beloved fellow believer to the teachings of the Holy Spirit. May we all, as we study his work, be partakers of the anointing which teaches all things.

Andrew Murray
Wellington, Cape of Good Hope
August 15, 1888

HOW TO READ THIS BOOK

This book is divided into 31 chapters that can be used as a daily devotional. It is recommended that the book be read and prayed through repeatedly. May the Lord Jesus Christ bless you as you take in his Spirit, the Spirit of Christ.

Before you begin each chapter please pray this prayer:

"Oh God and Father of our Lord Jesus Christ, I pray that you would give me a spirit of wisdom and revelation that I might understand the spiritual truths contained here by the leading and anointing of the Holy Spirit, who lives in me. Protect me, Father, from trying to understand spiritual truths with my natural mind. I know that the natural man cannot understand spiritual things. Therefore, I ask you for spiritual wisdom that I might understand spiritual things in my spirit. Thank you, Father. In Jesus I pray. Amen"

TABLE OF CONTENTS

CHAPTER 1

GOD'S SPIRIT, AND
A NEW SPIRIT

"A new heart also I will give you, and a new spirit I will put within you... And I will put My Spirit within you." Ezekiel 36:26-27

God has revealed himself to man in two great covenants. The first was the time of promise and preparation - the second is that of fulfillment and possession. In harmony with the differences of the two covenants there are differences in the dynamics of God's Spirit. In the old covenant, or Old Testament as we know it today, the Spirit of God came upon men and worked with them in special times and ways - working from above, outwardly, then within - the Spirit of *preparation*. In the new covenant, or New Testament, the Spirit enters them and dwells within - working from within, then outward, and upwards - the Spirit of *indwelling* and *inhabitation*. In the old we had the

Spirit of God, the Almighty and the Holy One - in the new we have the Spirit of the Father of the Lord Jesus Christ.

The difference between the two revelations of the Holy Spirit should not be regarded as if with the closing of the old covenant the former ceased, and there was no longer needed the work of preparation. This is not true. Just as there was in the old, anticipations of the indwelling of God's Spirit, so now in the new, the two dimensional work of the Spirit still continues. Due to a lack of knowledge, or lack of faith, a believer may even today barely get beyond the Old Testament measure of the Spirit's working. The indwelling Spirit has been given to every child of God, and yet he may experience very little of him beyond the first half of the promise, which is the new spirit given in regeneration, to *prepare* him for the Indwelling. He may know almost nothing of God's own Spirit as a living person within. The Spirit's work in convicting of sin and righteousness, and in his leading to repentance and faith, and the new life, is the work of *preparation*. The unique glory of the Holy Spirit is his divine personal indwelling in the heart of the believer, there to reveal the Father and the Son. It is only as believers have this revelation are they able to receive the fullness prepared for them in Christ.

In the book of Ezekiel we find a very powerful promise, the twofold blessing which God pours out through his Spirit. The first is, "*I will put a new spirit within you,*" (Ezekiel 36:26), meaning that man's own spirit is to be renewed and brought to life by the work of God's Spirit. Then there is the second blessing, "*I will put My Spirit within you,*" (Ezekiel 36:37), and God the Holy Spirit will dwell *in* that new spirit. Where God is to dwell, he must have a habitation. With Adam he had to create a body before he breathed the spirit of life into him. In Israel, the Tabernacle and the Temple had to be built and completed before God could come down and inhabit them. And now a new heart is given and a new spirit is put within us as the essential requirement of his own Spirit being given to dwell within us. We see this in David's prayer, *Create in me a clean heart, O God, and renew a right spirit within me!* Then, *Take not Your Holy Spirit from me,* (see Psalm 51:10, 11). Look at what is expressed in the words, *"That which is born of the Spirit is spirit,"* (John 3:6). The Holy Spirit creates the new spirit. So, the two are also distinguished, *God's Spirit bears witness with our spirits that we are the children of God!* (Romans 8:16). Our spirit is the renewed, regenerated spirit; dwelling in this renewed spirit, and yet separate from it, is God's Holy Spirit, witnessing within, without, and through it.

It is important for us to recognize the differences between the relationship of *regeneration of the spirit,* and *the indwelling of the Spirit.* Regeneration is the work of the Holy Spirit, by convicting us of sin, then leading us to repentance and faith in Christ, and then imparting in us a new nature. Through the Spirit, God fulfills the promise, *"I will put a new spirit within you."* The believer is now a child of God, and *ready* for the Holy Spirit to dwell in him. Then the faith of the child of God can claim the second half of the promise. However, as long as the believer only looks at regeneration and the renewal formed in his spirit, he will never come to the life of fullness meant for him. But when he accepts God's promise that there is something greater than even the new nature, something more wonderful than the inner temple, that there is the life of the Spirit of the Father and the Son to come and dwell within him, (see John 14:23), then his one great desire becomes to *know* the Holy Spirit completely. It is the Spirit's work to reveal to the believer how he works and what he demands; to know with the Spirit's indwelling, how he may experience the complete fullness and the revelation of the Son of God, the Lord Jesus Christ, within him.

So, are the two parts of God's promise - preparation and indwelling - fulfilled simultaneously, or successively? From God's perspective they are simultaneous, the Spirit is not divided. In giving the Spirit, God gives himself and all that he is, as it was on the day of Pentecost. The three thousand, (see Acts 2:37-41), received a new regenerated spirit, in repentance and faith. And on that same day, after they had been baptized, they received the indwelling Spirit as God's seal to their faith. Through the word of the disciples, the Holy Spirit came upon them and did a mighty work among them, changing their disposition, heart, and spirit. And with the power of the Spirit working in them, they then received the baptism of the Holy Spirit to abide in them.

Even today when the Spirit of God moves upon men, those born of God receive from the beginning of their new life the conscious sealing and indwelling of the Holy Spirit. Yet there are recorded in scripture varied circumstances in which the two halves of the promise are not as closely linked. This occurred with the believers in Samaria who were converted under Philip's preaching, (see Acts 8:1-17), and later with those Paul met at Ephesus, (see Acts 19:1-6). Each of these events seemed to repeat the experience of the apostles themselves. We regard them as regenerate men before Jesus's death, however it was only at Pentecost that the promise of *"He shall be in you!"* was fulfilled. What was seen in them, where the grace of the Spirit was divided into two separate manifestations, may still take place in our day.

However, today where God gives his Spirit, he is mostly known and experienced only as the Spirit of regeneration - his indwelling presence remains a mystery. In the gift of God, the Spirit of Christ in all his fullness within us is granted once for all as the indwelling Spirit, but he is received and possessed only by faith. When the spiritual life among believers is weak, or when neither the messages of the word, or the testimony of the believers reflects the truth of the promise of the indwelling Spirit, we shouldn't be surprised that even where God gives his Spirit he will only be known and experienced as the Spirit of regeneration.

It is generally recognized throughout the Church today that the Holy Spirit does not have the recognition that he deserves as the equal of the Father and the Son. He is not acknowledged as the only way which the Father and the Son can be known and possessed, or in whom the Church has her fullness in Christ. In the reformation, the gospel of the Lord Jesus Christ had to be defended from the terrible misconception which had made man's own righteousness the grounds of his acceptance by God. *It is by grace you are saved.* In the years that have followed, God has entrusted us to build and develop the foundation of the gospel through the revelation of the indwelling Spirit of Christ. We have rested too easily in what has been received. There are many who say, *"I think I understand the work of the Father and the Son, and I'm thankful for them, but I don't see the place that the Holy Spirit has."* The modern day children of God need the teaching that the Holy Spirit is himself God, and that he is the guiding and sanctifying power for each to receive the indwelling of Christ through the Spirit.

Let us unite with all who are crying out for God to reveal his Holy Spirit to the Church in power. May each believer experience the double promise - *"I will put a new spirit within you, and I will put My Spirit within you."* Pray that we may fully grasp the wonderful revelation and grace of the indwelling Spirit; that we would then turn ourselves inward and have our whole being opened up to the complete revelation of the Father's love and the grace of the Lord Jesus Christ.

"Within you! Within you!" This repeated word from Ezekiel is one of the key words of the new covenant. *"I will put My law into their hearts, and in their minds I will write them,"* (Hebrews 10:16). *"I will put My fear in their hearts, that they shall not depart from Me,"* (Jeremiah 32:40). God created man's heart to be his own dwelling place. But sin entered and polluted it. Four thousand years later God's Spirit desired and worked to regain possession. In the human life and death of Christ, God's redemption was accomplished, and the kingdom of God was established. Jesus said, *"The kingdom of God has come near you... the kingdom of God is within you."* (See Luke 10:9; 17:21). It is *within* we must look for the fulfillment of the new covenant - the covenant not of ordinances, but of life. In the power of an endless life the law and the fear of God are to be given in our hearts; the Spirit of Christ himself is to be *within us* as the power of our life, and the life of our life. The glory of Jesus Christ, the conqueror, is to be seen not only on the cross, or in the resurrection, or even on the throne. It is *in* our hearts. *Within us* is to be the true display of the reality and the glory of God's redemption. *Within us*, in the deepest places of our innermost being, is the hidden sanctuary where the ark of the covenant now rests - sprinkled with the blood

of Jesus. It contains the living law written by the indwelling Spirit, and where, through the Holy Spirit, the Father and the Son have now come to dwell. (See John 14:23).

PRAYER:

"Oh God, thank you for this double grace. Thank you for placing in me a new spirit, and for forming in me a holy temple for your Spirit to dwell in. And thank you that your wonderful presence has come to me, to reveal the Father and the Son.

"O my God! I pray that you would open my eyes for this mystery of your love. Let your words 'within you' bring me low before you, and may my one desire be to have my spirit become the worthy dwelling place of your Spirit.

"Father, I thank you that your Spirit dwells in me. I pray, let his indwelling be in power, in a living fellowship with you, in the growing experience of his renewing power, in the ever-fresh anointing that witnesses to his presence, the indwelling of the Lord Jesus Christ. May my daily walk be in the deepest reverence of his holy presence within me, and may I experience the manifest presence of all that he is. Amen."

CHAPTER 2

THE BAPTISM OF THE SPIRIT

And John bore witness saying... "I did not know Him, but He who sent me to baptize with water said to me, 'Upon whom you see the Spirit descending, and remaining on Him, this is He who baptizes with the Holy Spirit.'" John 1:32-33

There were two things that John the Baptist preached concerning the person of Jesus Christ - first that he was the Lamb of God that takes away the sin of the world, and second that he would baptize us with the Holy Spirit and fire. The blood of the Lamb and the baptism of the Holy Spirit were the two inseparable points of his preaching. The Church is without power, and the Lord Jesus is without glory in her, unless the blood as the foundation stone, and the Spirit as the cornerstone are fully proclaimed.

Regrettably, the full extent of John's revelation about the Son of God is not completely embraced today. It is easier to understand and accept the declaration that he is the Lamb of God, and that our pardon and peace come through his suffering and atonement, than the inward truth of the baptism and indwelling life of the Holy Spirit. The pouring out of the blood of Christ took place upon the earth and was visible and outward - it could be understood according to the patterns represented in the old covenant. However, the pouring out of the Spirit took place in heaven, and was a divine and hidden mystery. The shedding of the blood was for the ungodly and the rebellious - the gift of the Holy Spirit was for the believer, and the obedient disciple. We should not be surprised today that where redemption and forgiveness are preached, but the baptism of the Holy Spirit and its purposes within us are not, that there is such weakness of devotion towards the Lord Jesus Christ.

Yet the promises of the Old Testament was what God desired - his Spirit living within us. John knew this and did not preach the atoning Lamb without also proclaiming the fullness of our redemption, and how God's high purpose was to be fulfilled in us through the Spirit. Sin was not only guilt and condemnation, it was also defilement and death. It had earned not only the loss of God's favor, but it also made us unfit for his fellowship. And without his fellowship, God's love, which had created man for himself, could not be satisfied. God wanted to have us for himself; he wanted our hearts and affections, our innermost personality, our entire life to be a home for his love, and a Temple for his worship. John's message included both the beginning and the end of redemption. The blood of the Lamb was to cleanse God's Temple, and then restore his throne *within* the heart of man. Nothing less than the baptism and indwelling of the Holy Spirit would satisfy the heart of either God or man.

What the baptism of the Holy Spirit meant, Jesus himself was to be the pattern; he would only give to us what he himself had first received; because the Holy Spirit rested and remained on him, he could now baptize with the Spirit. And what did the Spirit's descending and abiding on him mean? He had been conceived and born of the Spirit, and through the power of the Spirit he had grown up a holy child and youth, and had entered into manhood free from sin. Then he came to John and submitted himself to the baptism of repentance in order to fulfill all righteousness. For his obedience in yielding to the leading of the Spirit, the Father rewarded him with his seal of approval, and gave him all the fullness of the power of heaven. Beyond what he had previously experienced, the Father's conscious indwelling presence and power took possession of him, and qualified him for his work. The leading and the power of the Holy Spirit became his even more consciously than before, (see Luke 4:1,14,22); he was now anointed with the Holy Spirit and power.

However, even though he was baptized in the Spirit himself, he could not yet baptize others. He had to first meet and overcome temptation in the power of his baptism, then he had to learn obedience and suffer, and through the Holy Spirit offer himself as a sacrifice unto God and his will. Only then would he once more receive the Holy Spirit as the reward of his obedience, (see Acts 2:33), but now with the power to baptize all who belonged to him.

What we see in Jesus teaches us what the baptism of the Holy Spirit is. It is not the grace through which we turn to God, or are born again by the Spirit. When Jesus reminded his disciples of John's prophecy, (see Acts 1:4), they had already received this grace. Their baptism with the Spirit meant something greater. It was to be the conscious presence of the resurrected Christ, back from heaven to dwell within their hearts, and their participation in the power of his resurrected life. It was to be a baptism of joy and power in their living union with Jesus. All that the Holy Spirit had been to Jesus when he was baptized, he was to be to them as well. They would receive his wisdom, courage, and holiness in a living union with him on the throne of glory. Through the Spirit the Son was to manifest himself to them, (John 14:21), and the Father and the Son would come to them and make them their home, their special dwelling place. (See John 14:23).

Upon whom you see the Spirit descending, and remaining on Him, this is He who baptizes with the Holy Spirit. This revelation must come to us as well as to John. For us to know the full meaning of the baptism of the Holy Spirit, and how we are to receive it, we must also see the one on whom the Spirit descended and remained.

We must *see* Jesus baptized with the Holy Spirit, and understand why *he needed it*, how he prepared for it, how he yielded to it, and how in its power he died his death and was raised again. What Jesus now has to give us he first received for himself; what he received for himself he now gives to us as our own. *Upon whom you see the Spirit descending, and remaining... this is He who baptizes with the Holy Spirit.*

However, there may be questions that need answered. Was the baptism of the Holy Spirit at Pentecost the complete fulfillment of the promise? Was it the only baptism of the Spirit given to the newly born Church? What about the coming of the Holy Spirit on the disciples in Acts 4, on the Samaritans in Acts 8, the Gentiles in the house of Cornelius in Acts 10, or the twelve disciples at Ephesus in Acts 19? Are these also to be regarded as separate fulfillments of the words, *He shall baptize you with the Holy Spirit?* Is the sealing of the Spirit given to each believer in regeneration to be regarded as his baptism of the Spirit? Or is the baptism of the Holy Spirit, as some say, a distinct and separate blessing to be received later? And is it a blessing given only once, or can it be repeated and renewed? Throughout this book we shall shed light through God's word that may help us resolve some of these questions. But it is very important that at the beginning we don't become too preoccupied with points of minor relevance. Instead, let's focus on the rich spiritual lessons from God about the teaching of the baptism of the Holy Spirit. There are two lessons specifically:

1.) The baptism of the Holy Spirit is the crown and glory of Jesus's work. We must know that we need it, and that we have it, if we are to live the life God desires of us. The Lord Jesus needed it, his disciples needed it, and we need it! For many believers it remains a grace whispered of, but not to be possessed or enjoyed. But it is so much more than the working of the Spirit in rebirth. It is the personal Spirit of Christ making himself present within us, abiding in our hearts in the full power of his glorified life. It is the Spirit of the life of Christ Jesus making us free from the law of sin and death, and through personal experience bringing us into the liberty from sin, which Christ redeemed us. It is the anointing with power to fill us with boldness in the presence of every danger, and give us the victory over the world and every enemy. It is the fulfillment of what God meant in his promise, *"I will dwell in them and walk in them."* Let us ask the Father to reveal to us all that his love is meant for us, until our souls are filled with the glory of the thought, *He baptizes with the Holy Spirit.*

2.) It is Jesus who baptizes. Whether we look upon this baptism as something we already have, which we want to understand better, or something we still must receive, we can all agree on this - it is only in Christ, in our union and obedience to him, that a baptized life can be received, maintained, or renewed. *"He that believes in me,"* Jesus said, *"out of his innermost being shall flow rivers of living water."* (John 7:38 NASB). We need a living faith in the indwelling Jesus for the living waters to freely flow. Faith is the instinct of the new nature that recognizes and receives its divine food and drink. Through faith, let us trust Jesus, who baptizes and fills us with the Holy Spirit. In our union with him, and in the confidence that he has given himself to us fully, let us look to him for nothing less than all that the baptism of the Holy Spirit offers.

In doing so let's specifically remember one thing - only he that is faithful in the least will be made ruler over much. Be very faithful to what you already have and know of the Spirit's working. Regard yourself with deep reverence as God's holy Temple. Wait for and listen to the gentlest whispering of God's Spirit within you. Listen especially to your conscience, which has been cleansed in the blood of Christ - keep your conscience clean through simple childlike obedience. In your heart there still may be involuntary sin, and you may feel yourself powerless to overcome it. Humble yourself deeply over your inbred corruption, strengthened as it has been by actual sin. Confess every manifestation of such sin, and turn it over to the Lord Jesus to be cleansed in the blood.

But in regard to your daily conscious actions, declare to the Lord Jesus Christ that you will do everything that you know you should do in order to be pleasing to him. Yield to the convictions of your conscience when you fail. Do not give up, and do not lose hope in God. Renew your vow, *"What I know God wants me to do,*

I will do." Humbly do this every morning and wait for the Spirit's leading; his voice will gradually become better known, and his strength will be felt. Jesus had his disciples for three years in his Holy Spirit baptism class, and then the blessing came. Let us be his obedient disciples and students, and believe in him on whom the Spirit abides, and who is full of the Spirit. And we too will become prepared for the full grace of the baptism of the Holy Spirit.

PRAYER:

"Blessed Lord Jesus! I worship you with my whole heart, and I ask you to baptize me with the Holy Spirit. O Lord, reveal yourself to me in this your glory, that I may rightly know what I can expect from you.

"I bless you that I am being prepared to receive the Holy Spirit in his fullness. During your whole life of preparation for your work in Nazareth the Spirit was always in you. And yet when you had surrendered yourself to fulfill all righteousness, and to enter into fellowship with the sinners you came to save, in participating in their baptism of repentance, you received from the Father a new infilling of his Holy Spirit. It was to you the seal of his love, and the revelation of his indwelling, and the power for his service. And now we ask you to do for us what the Father did for you.

"My Holy Lord, I bless you that the Holy Spirit is in me too! But I ask you for more, that you would give me the full and overflowing measure that you have promised. Let him be to me the full unceasing revelation of your presence in my heart, as glorious and mighty as you are on the throne of heaven. Lord Jesus! Baptize me and fill me with your precious Holy Spirit! Amen."

CHAPTER 3

WORSHIP IN THE SPIRIT

"But the hour is coming, and now is, when the true worshipers will worship the Father in spirit and truth; for the Father is seeking such to worship Him. God is Spirit, and those who worship Him must worship in spirit and truth." John 4:23-24

For we are the circumcision, which worship God in the Spirit, and rejoice in Christ Jesus, and have no confidence in the flesh. Philippians 3:3

Man was created by God for fellowship, and worship is that fellowship's divine expression; to worship God is man's highest honor and glory. All of the exercises of a believer's life - meditation and prayer, love and faith, surrender and obedience - culminate in worship. As I recognize the holiness, the glory, and the love of God, and as I realize my own sinful nature and the Father's kind redemption, I present my whole being unto God in worship. I offer him, in humility and adoration, the glory that is due him alone. The most complete approach to God is in worship. Every sentiment, service and aspect of the believer's life is included in it. Worship is man's highest destiny, because in it God is all in all.

Jesus declared that with his coming a new type of worship would begin. Everything that the Gentiles or Samaritans had called worship, even what the Jews knew of it according to the law of Moses, would make way for something entirely new: worship in spirit and in truth, released through the giving of the Holy Spirit. This is now the only worship which is well pleasing to the Father. It is for this reason that we have received the Holy Spirit. The primary purpose of the Holy Spirit within us is so that we worship God in spirit and in truth. *"For the Father seeks such to worship Him"* - this is why he sent forth his Son and his Spirit.

In Spirit - God created man as a living soul, and the soul as the center of man's personality and consciousness. It was linked on one side through the body to the outer visible world, and on the other side through the spirit to the divine, the unseen God. The soul had to decide whether it would yield itself to the spirit, linked to God and his will, or to the body and its natural desires. When man fell the soul refused the rule of the spirit, and became the slave of the body with all its demands and appetites. Man became *flesh,* and the spirit lost its destined place of rule, becoming little more than a dormant power, no longer the ruling principle, but a struggling captive. Now the spirit stands in hostility to the *flesh,* which is the life of the soul and the body, now joined together in captivity to sin.

When speaking of the unregenerate man in contrast with the spiritual, (see 1 Corinthians 2:14), Paul called him soulish, having only the natural life. The life of the soul discerns all of our moral and intellectual qualities, even the things of God, but does so apart from the new birth. Because the fallen soul is under the power of the flesh, man is spoken of as having become *flesh,* or as *being flesh.* As the body consists of flesh and bone, and the flesh is that part of it which is specifically endowed with sensitivity, through which we receive our sensations from the outer world, the flesh represents our human nature now subject to the world of senses. And because the soul has come under the power of the flesh, the scriptures speak of all the attributes of the soul as belonging to the *flesh,* and being under its power. So there is now a contrast between the flesh and the spirit regarding the things of God. There is *fleshly* wisdom and *spiritual* wisdom (1 Corinthians 2:12; Colossians 1:9); service to God that trusts in the flesh and revels in the flesh, and service to God by the spirit, (see Philippians 3:3; Galatians 6:13). There is a *fleshly* mind and a *spiritual* mind (see Colossians 1:9, 2:18). There is the will of the flesh, and a will which is of God working by his Spirit, (see John 1:13; Philippians 2:13). And there is worship which is satisfying to the flesh, because it is in the power of what the flesh can do, (see Colossians 2:18, 23), and there is a worship of God which is in the Spirit. This last one is the worship that Jesus came to reveal by giving a new spirit in our inner man, and within that spirit his coming as the Holy Spirit.

'In Spirit and *Truth.'* Worship in spirit is worship in truth. The words *in spirit* do not mean internal versus external observances, or hearty, sincere, or upright, but rather spiritual, placed there by God's Spirit, the opposite of what man's natural power can affect. In the worship of the old covenant the people knew that God desired truth in their inner being. Even though they sought him with their whole hearts they did not understand worship in spirit and in truth. *Truth* here means the substance, the reality and the actual possession of all that the worship of God implies, both in its demands and its promises. John speaks of Jesus as *the only begotten of the Father, full of grace and truth,* (see John 1:16, 17). If we consider truth as the opposite of falsehood, the law of Moses was just as true as the Gospel of Jesus - they both came from God. But if we realize that the law gave only a shadow of *good things to come,* and that Christ brought us the substance of the things themselves, we see how he was full of truth, because he *is* truth. He is the reality and the life, the love and the power, in the *truth* of God revealing itself to us. Only a worship *in spirit* can be a worship *in truth.* It is the Holy Spirit who reveals this to us, and preserves it within us.

"*The true worshippers worship the Father in spirit and in truth.*" Not all who worship are true worshippers. There may be much singing, music, and energy in trying to worship God without it being worship in spirit and truth. The mind, will, and emotions may be intensely engaged, and feelings may be deeply stirred, but still limited spiritual worship in the truth of God. There may be great connection to biblical truth, and yet the predominate activity comes from man's own efforts, not the Spirit's work - it is not the worship that God seeks. There must be conformity and unity between God, who is the Spirit, and his worshippers who draw near in the Spirit. These are the ones the Father seeks to worship him. The infinite and perfect Holy Spirit, which God the Father is, must be reflected in the spirit which is in the child; this can only be true as the Spirit of God dwells in us.

If we would seek to become true worshippers in spirit and in truth, we must sense the danger that we are in from the *flesh* and all its forms of worship. We who believe have in us a double nature - flesh and spirit. One is the natural part, always ready to insert itself and take over doing what is needed in the worship of God - the other is the spiritual part, which may still be very weak; we may not even know yet how to give it full control. Our minds and emotions may delight and be moved by the word of God, and our will may see in Romans 7:22, *delight in the law of God after the inward man,* and yet we may be powerless to keep that law, and to render to God the obedience and worship we know he requires.

We need the Holy Spirit's indwelling for both life and worship. But to receive this the flesh must be silenced. *Be silent, all flesh, before the Lord. Let no flesh glory in His presence,* (Zechariah 2:13). The Father had already revealed to Peter, through the Spirit, that Jesus was the Christ, and yet Peter could not grasp the thought of the cross. His mind was not given to the things of God, but to the natural interest of men. (See Matthew 16:16-17, 21-23). We must give up our own thoughts regarding the things of God, and our own efforts to wake up, or work up the right feelings to worship - our natural ability to worship must be relinquished, and every approach to God must be in quiet surrender to the Holy Spirit. It is impossible for the Spirit to work in us through our own will. If we seek to worship in the spirit, we must walk in the spirit. *You are not in the flesh but in the spirit, if indeed the Spirit of God dwells in you,* (Romans 8:9). As the Spirit dwells and rules in me, then I am in the spirit, and I can indeed worship in the spirit.

"*The hour comes, and now is, when the true worshippers shall worship the Father in spirit and in truth; for the Fathers seeks such as these to be His worshippers.*" And what the Father seeks, he will always find, for he is the one who calls us. Christ came to seek and save us, that we would become the true worshippers the Father longs for. We are able worship God through the torn veil of the flesh of Jesus, and then the Spirit of Christ comes to us, to be in us the truth and the reality of his presence, and to communicate within us his very own life. Praise the Lord! The hour has come, and now is - we are living in it this very moment - that the true worshippers shall worship the Father in Spirit and in Truth. Let us believe it! The Spirit has been given and dwells within us for this one purpose: the Father seeks such worshippers. Let's rejoice in the confidence that we can obtain it; we can be true worshippers because the Holy Spirit has been given to us.

Finally, let us realize in the holy fear and awe of the Lord that he dwells within us. Let's humbly silence our flesh, and yield ourselves to his leading and teaching. Let's wait in faith before God for his workings, and let's practice this worship. Let every new insight into what the work of the Spirit means, let every exercise of faith in his indwelling, or the experience of his working, end in this as its highest glory: that we would worship the Father, giving to him the praise and thanksgiving, and the honor and love which are his alone. Let us do this in spirit and truth.

PRAYER:

"*Oh God! You are Spirit, and they that worship you must worship you in spirit and truth. Blessed be your name! You sent your own Son to redeem us and prepare us for worship in the spirit, and you sent forth your Spirit to dwell in us and make us ready for this. And now we have access to you, Father, through the Son, and in the Spirit.*

"Father, we confess with shame how much our worship has been in the power and the will of the flesh. We have dishonored you, and have grieved your Holy Spirit, and brought infinite loss to our souls. Oh God, forgive us and save us from this sin. Teach us to never attempt to worship you except in spirit and truth.

"Lord, your Holy Spirit dwells in us. We ask you, according to the riches of your glory, to strengthen us with his power, that our inner man may indeed be a spiritual temple, where spiritual sacrifices are unceasingly offered. And teach us the blessed art, as often as we enter your presence, of yielding self and the flesh to the death, and waiting for and trusting the Spirit who is in us, to work in us a worship and faith and love, which are acceptable to you through the Lord Jesus Christ. And Father, we pray that throughout your worldwide Church, a worship in spirit and truth may be sought after, reached, and given to you every day. We ask all this in the name of Jesus, our Lord. Amen."

CHAPTER 4

THE SPIRIT AND THE WORD

"It is the Spirit who gives life; the flesh profits nothing. The words that I speak to you are Spirit and they are Life..." "Lord, to whom shall we go? You have the words of eternal life." John 6:63, 68

Who also made us sufficient as ministers of the new covenant, not of the letter but of the Spirit; for the letter kills, but the Spirit gives life. 2 Corinthians 3:6

The Lord Jesus, speaking about himself as the bread of life, and of his flesh and blood as the meat and drink of eternal life, was a hard saying that many of his disciples could not understand or accept. Jesus tells them that it is only when the Holy Spirit has come, and they have him, that his words will become clear to them. He says, *"It is the Spirit who gives life; the flesh profits nothing; the words that I speak to you are Spirit and they are Life,"* (John 6:63).

"It is the Spirit who gives life." In these words of Christ, and similar words from Paul, *the Spirit gives life,* we have the closest to a definition of the Spirit. (Compare to 1 Corinthians 15:45, *a life-giving Spirit.*). First, and this is important: the Spirit always acts as a *life-giver,* whether in nature or in grace. His work in the believer of sealing, sanctifying, enlightening, and strengthening, are all rooted in it. It is only as he is known and honored, and waited on in the inner life of the soul, that his other graces can be fully experienced. They are the outgrowth and the power of the life within. *"It is the Spirit that gives life..."*

In contrast to the Spirit, the Lord says, *"the flesh profits nothing."* He is not speaking about the flesh as the origin of sin, but of its religious form. The flesh is the power through which the natural man seeks to serve God, or to know the things of God. Jesus summed up its fruitless efforts with the words, *"the flesh profits nothing."* Everything that stems from the flesh is useless in teaching the spiritual life and the things of God. Paul says the same thing when he compares the Spirit with *the letter that kills,* (See 2 Corinthians 3:6). The old covenant was the dispensation of *the letter of the law* and the *flesh.* Even though it had a certain glory, and Israel's privileges were very great, Paul said, *For indeed what had glory, in this case has no glory because of the glory that has surpassed it,* (2 Corinthians 3:10 NASB). Even Christ's own words did not have the desired effect in his disciples while he was still in his human body. It was only in the tearing of the veil of his flesh - his death - that the new disposition of the Spirit took the place of the flesh.

"It is the Spirit who gives life, the flesh profits nothing. The words that I have spoken to you, they are Spirit and they are Life," (John 6:63). In these words Jesus wishes to teach his disciples two things: *first,* his words are powerful living seeds which will grow up *in* us, proclaiming and revealing their meaning and power in those who receive them in the heart. He did not want them to be discouraged if they could not initially understand them. His words are spirit and life. They aren't meant for the natural understanding, but for the *life.* They enter into the roots of life through the power of the

unseen Spirit, which is higher, and deeper than all thought. They have a divine life and work with a divine energy to bring their truth into the experience of those who receive them. *Second*, a good seed needs good soil; there must be life in the soil as well as in the seed. The word cannot be kept alone in the mind, will, or feelings, but must pass *through them* into the *life*. The center of that *life* is man's spiritual nature. There the authority of the word must be recognized, with the conscience as its voice. It is only as the Holy Spirit becomes our life, can we receive the words of God, and activate them in us as truth and the power in us.

In our study of the work of the Holy Spirit, we cannot be careful enough to get hold of this truth. It will save us from both *right-handed* and *left-handed* errors; *right hand*, the teaching of the Spirit without the word of God, and *left hand,* the teaching of the word of God without the Spirit.

First, we have the *right-hand* error - seeking the teaching of the Spirit without the word. In the three persons of God, the Word (Christ) and the Spirit are always in each other, and are one with the Father. It is no different with the God-inspired words of the bible. Throughout time the Holy Spirit has expressed the thoughts of God in the written words of the scriptures. And he now lives in our hearts for this purpose, to reveal the power and the meaning of the word to us. If you desire to be full of the Holy Spirit, then be full of the word of God. If you desire for the divine life of the Spirit to become strong within you, and to acquire power in every part of your life, then let the word of Christ dwell in you richly. If you want the Spirit to be your helper in recalling and applying the words of Jesus that he spoke regarding your needs at the moment you need them, then have the words of Christ abiding in you. If you want the Spirit to reveal to you the will of God in each cir-cumstance of life, showing you the correct path or choice to take, or make, in the middle of what seems like conflicting thoughts or ideas, at the moment you need it, then have the words of Christ living in you. Finally, if you want God's word as your light, let the written word be written on your heart *by the Holy Spirit*. "*The Words that I speak to you, they are Spirit and Life*" Take them and treasure them; it is through them that the Spirit makes known and reveals his life's power.

Second, we have the *left-handed,* and more common error. The word of God cannot release its life in you apart from the Spirit of God within you accepting and appropriating it in your inner life. How much scripture reading, bible study, and preaching goes on today where the primary objective is to reach the exact and precise meaning of the written word? Many think that if they know correctly what it means, even going back to the original language, they will receive the precise understanding, and the blessing the word is meant to bring. That is not true. The word is like a seed, unless it is exposed to good soil and the sun and water, the life in it may never grow. Likewise, we may hold the words and doctrines of the scriptures very clearly in our minds, yet know very little of their true life and power. We need to constantly remind ourselves, and the body of Christ, that the scriptures which were spoken and written by holy men of old, as they were moved by the Holy Spirit, can only be understood today by holy men and women, as they are moved and taught by the same Holy Spirit. "*The words I have spoken... are spirit and life.*" In our taking them in and feeding on them, we know that "*the flesh profits nothing, it is the Spirit that gives life,*" the Spirit of life *within* us.

This is one of the sober lessons which the Jews in the time of Christ teach us. They were zealous for God's word and his honor, but it was only for their human interpretation of it that they were zealous. Jesus said to them, "*You search the scriptures, for in them you think you have eternal life; and these are they which testify of Me. But you are not willing to come to Me that you may have life,*" (John 5:39-40). They trusted in the scriptures to lead them to eternal life, but they couldn't see that those same scriptures testified of Jesus, so they did not come to him. They studied and accepted the scriptures only with the light and the power of their natural human understanding, not in the light and power of God's Spirit. Many believers today are weak; even though they read and know the scriptures they do not understand that it is only the Spirit that gives life and revelation to them. Their natural understanding, regardless of how intelligent, educated, or sincere they are, profits them nothing. Like the Jews, they think that in the scriptures they have eternal life, but they know little or nothing of the living Christ through the power of the Holy Spirit in them.

We must be determined to avoid all attempts to study or use the written word of God without the life-giving power of the Holy Spirit. Let us never take scripture into our hands, or our minds, or our mouth, without accepting the need and the promise of the Spirit. In *worship,* look to God to give and renew the workings of his Spirit within you. Then in *faith*, yield yourself to the power that lives in you; wait on him, that you may be opened to receive the word, not only with your mind, but through the *life* that is in you. Let the Holy Spirit be your life. As the Spirit *within* comes out and meets the word from *without* as its food, then the words of Christ are indeed Spirit and Life within.

As the Lord's words are Spirit and Life, it becomes very clear that the Spirit in us must be the Spirit of our life. Deeper down than our mind, or feelings, or our will, down to their roots and motivations, down there must be the Spirit of God. As we go lower than these we see that nothing equals the Spirit of Life which lies within the words of the Living God. Let us wait on the Holy Spirit in the unseen depths of the hidden life. As we receive his words of life-giving power and work them into the life of our life, we will know what it means in truth, *"It is the Spirit that gives Life."* We will see how God's will is revealed when the words which are Spirit and Life are met and greeted in us by the Spirit and Life dwelling *within*. They alone will release their meaning and impart their substance, giving us their divine strength and fullness to the Spirit and the Life already within.

PRAYER:

"Oh my God, thank you again for the wonderful gift of your indwelling Spirit. And I humbly ask you again that I may indeed know that he is in me, and the glorious divine work that he is carrying on. Teach me to believe that he is the life

and the strength of the growth of the divine life within me, and the pledge and assurance that I can grow up into all that my God would have me become. As I see this I will understand how he, as the Spirit of Life within me, will make my spirit hunger for the word of God as the food of life, and I will receive it and assimilate it, and it will indeed become my life and power.

"Forgive me, Lord, for seeking to understand your words, which are Spirit and Life, in the power of my human thoughts and my fleshly mind. I have been so slow to learn that the flesh truly profits nothing. I desire to learn this now.

"Father, grant me the Spirit of Wisdom and Revelation, and please grant me the mighty workings of the Spirit, that I may know how deeply spiritual each word of yours is, and how spiritual things can only be spiritually discerned. Teach me in all of my fellowship with your word to deny my flesh and my natural mind, and to wait in deep humility and faith for the inward working of the Spirit to give life to the Word. May all of my meditations of your Word, and all of my keeping of it in faith and obedience, be in Spirit and in Truth, and in Life and Power. Amen!"

CHAPTER 5

THE GLORIFIED JESUS

On the last day, that great day of the feast, Jesus stood and cried out, saying "If anyone thirst, let him come to Me and drink. He who believes in Me, as the Scripture has said, out of his heart will flow rivers of living water." But this He spoke concerning the Spirit, whom those believing in Him would receive; for the Holy Spirit was not yet given, because Jesus was not yet glorified. John 7:37-39

Jesus promised here that those who come to him and drink, who believe in him, will not only never thirst again, but will themselves become fountains of living water streaming forth rivers of life and blessing. John explains in these verses that the promise was a future one that would only be fulfilled after the Spirit was poured out. The reason for this delay was the Holy Spirit had not yet been given, because Jesus was not yet glorified. The original expression was *the Spirit was not yet,* however, because this sounded strange, the word *given* has been inserted. But the original expression may actually guide us into the true understanding of the significance of the Spirit's not coming until Jesus was glorified.

We have seen that God has given us a twofold revelation of himself, first as God in the old testament, then as Father in the new. The Son, who had been with the Father for eternity, entered a new stage of existence when he became flesh. After his return to heaven he was still the only begotten Son of God, and yet he was not entirely the same. He was now also the Son of Man, the first-born from the dead, clothed with a glorified humanity that he had perfected and sanctified for himself. The Spirit of God, likewise, as he was poured out on the day of Pentecost, was also something new. Throughout the old testament he was always called the Spirit of God, or the Spirit of the Lord; the name Holy Spirit was not yet known. Only in his work of preparing the way for Christ, and in preparing a body for him, does his proper name come into use, (see Luke 1:15, 35). When poured out at Pentecost, he came as the Spirit of the glorified Jesus, the Spirit of the incarnate, crucified and exalted Christ. He was the bearer and communicator to us of *Life* as it had been interwoven into human nature in the person of Jesus Christ.

It is in this capacity that he bears the name of Holy Spirit, for it is as the indwelling one that God is holy. The Son of Man became the Son of God. The Holy Spirit is the Spirit of the glori-fied Jesus; he could not come, and he could not indwell us until Jesus had been glorified.

The Holy Spirit that has been sent to dwell in us is not the Spirit of God as such, but *the Spirit of Jesus*. Sin not only disturbed our relationship to God's perfect law, but to God himself. With the loss of divine favor we also lost the divine life. The Lord Jesus Christ did not come back just to deliver man from the law and its curse, but to bring mankind itself back into the fellowship of the divine life, as participants of the divine nature. He could not do this by an exercise of divine power over man, but only in the path of a free, moral and human development. In his own existence in the flesh he sanctified it and made it a fit and willing receptacle for the indwelling of the Spirit of God. Then in death he became both the curse for sin, and the seed to bring forth fruit in us. As he was glorified in the resurrection and the ascension, his spirit came forth as the spirit of his human life. It was glorified into union with his divine nature, that we might participate in him and his glorified life. Because of his death on the cross as the Son of Man, mankind now had the right and the title to the fullness of the Holy Spirit, the Spirit of the glorified Christ, and to his indwelling life.

By perfecting in himself a new and holy human nature on our behalf, he could now communicate what previously did not exist, a life that is both human and divine. Therefore the Holy Spirit, as he was the personal divine life of Jesus, could also be the same in the personal life of men. He is the personal life principle of the Lord Jesus Christ, and he can be the same in the child of God; the Spirit of God's Son can now be the Spirit that cries out in our hearts, *"Abba, Father!"* (See Romans 8:15; Galatians 4:5). We can now understand what John meant when he wrote, *The Spirit was not yet, because Jesus was not yet glorified.*

Since Jesus has now been glorified, the promise can be fulfilled, *"He that believes on Me, out of him shall flow rivers of living waters."* The great transaction which took place when Jesus was glorified, is now an eternal reality. When Christ became flesh and entered into our human nature, there took place in the Holiest of All what Peter said, *Being exalted at the right hand of God, He received from the Father the promise of the Holy Spirit,* (Acts 2:33). As man, and the head of man, he was admitted into the full glory of the divine, and his human nature became the receptacle and the dispenser of the Spirit. The Holy Spirit could come down as the Spirit of the God-man, fully the Spirit of God, and fully the spirit of man. He could be in each one who believes in Jesus, the Spirit of God's personal life and presence, and at the same time the spirit of the personal life of the believer. In Christ the perfect union of God and man was achieved. When he sat down upon the throne, he did so in a new form of existence, a glory previously unknown. So too, a new era began in the life and the work of the Spirit. He now comes as the witness to the perfect union of the divine and the human, and in becoming our life we participate in it. He has poured forth the Spirit of the glorified Jesus, and has streamed *into* us and *through* us, to stream forth *from* us in rivers of blessing.

The glorifying of Jesus, and the streaming forth of his Spirit, are in union, and inseparably linked together. We receive not only the Spirit of God, but the Spirit of the glorified Jesus - this is the Spirit which was not yet. It is especially with the glorified Jesus that we must believe in and embrace. We must not be content only with the faith that trusts in the cross and its pardon. As great as that is, we must also seek to know the new life of glory and divine power in human nature. This is what the Holy Spirit, the Spirit of the glorified Jesus, is meant to bear witness to. It is the mystery that was hidden throughout the ages, but is now made known by the Holy Spirit: Christ in us, living out his divine life in us who are in the flesh. We have the most intense personal interest in knowing and understanding what it means that Jesus is glorified. Not just because we will see and share in his glory, but we are to live in it even now on a daily basis. The Holy Spirit is able to *be* to us just as much as we are willing to *have* of him and of the life of the glorified Lord.

This He spoke concerning the Spirit, whom those believing in Him would receive; for the Holy Spirit was not yet, because Jesus was not yet glorified. In the Old Testament, when the Spirit was mentioned, it was always as God's Spirit, and the power with which he was working. In the new testament the Spirit was not yet known on the earth as a person. At Pentecost the Holy Spirit descended as a person to dwell in us, and the trinity of God was revealed. This is the fruit of Jesus's work, that we now have the personal presence of the Holy Spirit on earth. Jesus came as the second person, to reveal the Father, and the Father dwelt in him. Likewise, the Spirit comes as the third person, to reveal the Son, and in him the Son dwells, and works in us. This is the glory in which the Father glorifies the Son of Man, because the Son had glorified him. And through the Son, the Holy Spirit descends as a person to dwell in believers, and to make the glorified Jesus a present reality within them. He is the one whom Jesus spoke, "*whoever believes in Me shall never thirst, but shall have rivers of living water flowing out of him."* This is the only thing that can satisfy the soul's thirst and make it a life-giving fountain for others: the personal indwelling of the Holy Spirit, revealing the presence of the glorified Jesus.

"He that believes in Me, rivers of living water shall flow out of him." This he spoke of the Spirit... This is the key to unlocking all of God's treasures, *"He that believes in Me."* Let us believe in the glorious Jesus who baptizes with the Holy Spirit.

Through the riches of his glory God has given us his Holy Spirit that we would have his presence within us, and as we believe and accept his Spirit, he works in us and through us. By faith the glory of Jesus in heaven, and the power of the Spirit in our hearts, have become inseparably linked. Let us believe that as we fellowship with Jesus, rivers of living water will flow into us and out of us as an increasing stream.

Yes, believe on the Lord Jesus, but please remembers this - faith means absolute surrender to God. Believing is the power of the renewed nature which is willing to forsake self, and die to it, to make room for the Holy Spirit as the glorified Christ, to come and take possession of us, and do his work through us. Faith in Jesus bows low in humility and poverty of spirit. It realizes that self has nothing, and that another, the unseen Spirit, now has come to be its leader, strength and life. Faith in Jesus bows in the stillness of a quiet surrender before him, fully assured that as it waits on him, he will cause the river to flow.

PRAYER:

"Blessed Lord Jesus, I believe! Help me overcome my unbelief! You are the author and the perfecter of my faith; perfect the work of faith in me. Teach me, O Lord, with a faith that enters the unseen, that I might realize what your glory is, and what my share is in it.

"Lord Jesus, you said, 'The glory which you gave me, I have given them.' Teach me that the Holy Spirit and his power is the glory which you gave us, and that you would have us manifest your glory as we rejoice in his holy presence on earth and his

indwelling in us. Teach me, above all Lord, to not take and hold these blessed truths only in my mind, but also with my spirit that is in my inward most parts, to wait on you that I might be filled with your Spirit.

"O Lord, I bow before your glory in humble faith. Let all of my life of self and the flesh be exposed and perish, as I worship and wait before you. Let the Spirit of Glory become my life, let his presence break down all my trust in myself and make room for you. And let my whole life be lived out in the faith of the Son of God, who loved me and gave himself up for me. Amen."

CHAPTER 6

THE INDWELLING SPIRIT

"And I will pray the Father, and He will give you another Helper, that He may abide with you forever - the Spirit of Truth, whom the world cannot receive, because it neither sees Him nor knows Him; but you know Him, for He dwells with you and will be in you." John 14:16 - 17

"*He will be in you.*" In these five simple words the Lord Jesus announces the wonderful mystery of the Holy Spirit's indwelling, which is the fruit and the crown of his redeeming work. It was for this purpose that man had been created. It was for this, God's mastery within the human heart, that the Spirit had labored in vain within us through the past ages. And this was the reason Jesus had come as a man, and was about to die. Without this the Father's purpose and his own work would fail. It was because the Spirit did not yet indwell them, that the Lord's interaction with his disciples had such little effect. He rarely mentioned it to them because he knew they couldn't understand. But on the last night during his final moments before the cross, he disclosed the divine secret: when he left them their loss would be replaced by something far greater than his bodily presence. Another would come in his place and abide with them forever, and would dwell *in* them. And by dwelling in them, the Spirit would prepare them to receive Jesus himself again, along with the Father. *'He shall be in you.'* (See John 14:23).

The Father has given us a two dimensional revelation of himself. In Jesus Christ, the Son, he reveals his holy image, and setting him before men he invites them to become like him by receiving him into their hearts and life. Through his Spirit he sends forth his divine power to enter into us, and from within prepares us to receive both the Son and the Father. The dispensation of the Spirit is the dispensation of the inner life. The dispensation of the Word, or the Son, began with the creation of man in God's own image, and continued through all of the preparatory stages right down to Christ's appearing in the flesh. This was an external preparation. At times there were special and powerful workings of the Spirit that still needed to be completed. Eternal life was to become the very life of man, hiding itself within his being and consciousness, and clothing itself in the forms of the human life and will. Just as it is through the Spirit that God is what he is, and just as the Spirit is the principle of the personalities and character of the Father and the Son, so also the Holy Spirit is now to be in us, the principle of our life, and the root of our personality and character - the life of our entire being and consciousness. He is to be one with us in the perfection of a divine life dwelling in us, even as the Father is in the Son, and the Son is in the Father.

If we are to enter into the full understanding and experience of what the Lord Jesus promises here, we must remember that what he is speaking of is a divine indwelling. Wherever God dwells he hides himself. In nature he hides himself, most won't see him there. In his meetings with the saints of old he usually hid himself under some manifestation of human weakness. It was often only after he was gone that they said, *Surely the Lord was in this place, and we did not know it.* The Son came to reveal God, and yet he came as a root out of dry ground, without a beautiful appearance or character. At times, even his own disciples were offended by him. Men always expect the kingdom of God to come with observation; they do not understand that it is a hidden mystery, to be received only as God makes himself known within hearts that are surrendered, and made ready for him. When the Holy Spirit occupies them, believers invariably seem to believe that his leading can be known in their thoughts, that his life in them will affect their feelings, and his sanctifying work can be recognized in their will and conduct. They must be reminded that deeper than their mind, feelings, and will, deeper down than the soul - in the depths of the spirit that is from God - there the Holy Spirit dwells.

The initial, and continuous indwelling, can only be recognized by faith. Even when I cannot see any evidence of his working, by faith I believe that he dwells in me. In faith I rest and wait in trust as he works in me. In faith I must deny my own wisdom and strength, and depend upon him to work. His first workings within me may be so faint and hidden that I hardly recognize them as coming from him. They may appear to be nothing more than the voice of conscience, or the familiar sound of some bible truth. This is when faith holds fast to the promise of the Father's gift, and trusts that the Spirit is within us, and will guide us. In faith I will continue to yield my whole life and being to his rule, and I will be faithful to what appears to be the nearness of his voice. With faith such as this, my soul will learn to recognize his voice better. Rising out of my hidden depths, his power will move to take possession of my mind and will, and his indwelling presence in the hidden recesses of my heart will grow, and I will come into his fullness.

Faith is the one quality of our spiritual nature through which we can recognize God, regardless of how he may reveal himself. If this is true of the Father in his glory as God, and true of the Son as the manifestation of the Father, it is equally true of the Spirit, the unseen divine life and power of the Son, who has come to clothe and hide himself within our weakness. Let us cultivate and exercise our faith in the Father, whose gift through the Son is this - the Spirit is in our hearts. The whole person, and the work and the glory of the Son is contained in the gift of the indwelling Holy Spirit. So, let our faith grow strong in the unseen, sometimes unfelt, presence of his mighty power. The Spirit is a living person who has descended into our weakness and hidden himself in our smallness, to prepare us to become the dwelling place of the Father and the Son. The seal of our acceptance, and the promise of a deeper and richer knowledge of God, is this: *the Holy Spirit dwells in you.*

The deep importance of the indwelling of the Spirit is evident from the place it occupies in the Lord's final words to his disciples. In John 14, and the two following chapters, he speaks of the Spirit more directly as teacher and witness, representing and glorifying himself, and convicting the world. During this same address he connects the indwelling of the Father and the Son, (see John 14:23), with the union of the vine and the branches, (John 15). He also speaks of the peace, joy, and the power in prayer that his disciples would have in the day of the Spirit's coming - *"The Spirit shall be in you."* Jesus wanted his disciples, and us, to know that it is only as the indwelling Spirit, that he can be our teacher and our strength. As we accept his words, *"He shall be in you,"* and live under the control of this faith, our true relationship with the Holy Spirit will be realized. He will take charge and powerfully fill and bless the one who is surrendered to him as his home, and his special dwelling place.

A careful study of Paul's letters will confirm this. In First Corinthians, he had to reprimand them for their terrible sins, and yet he says to them all, including the weakest and the most unfaithful believer, *Do you not know that your body is the Temple of the Holy Spirit who is in you, whom you have received from God?* (1 Corinthians 6:19). He was sure that if they believed this, and if this truth was given the place that God meant for it to have, it would be the motive and the power of a new and holy life. To the deceived Galatians, he reminded them that they had received the Spirit only by faith. God had sent forth the Spirit of his Son into their hearts, and they had life only through the Spirit who lived in them. If they were to believe and live in the Spirit, then they could also walk in the Spirit.

The Church today still needs this teaching. I am convinced that very few of us understand this truth concerning the Holy Spirit, or to what extent this is the cause of our own weakness. There may be correct preaching, and absolute dependence in prayer for the Holy Spirit to work, but unless his personal and divine indwelling is acknowledged and experienced, there will be continual failure. He wants his resting place free from all intrusions and disturbances. God wants the entire possession of his temple - Jesus wants his home all to himself. He cannot do his work there, to rule and reveal himself and his love as he would, unless the whole house, the inner being, has been possessed and filled by the Holy Spirit.

Let us agree to seek this. As the meaning of the indwelling dawns upon us in its fullness, as we accept it in faith, to be accomplished and maintained only in God's power; and as we empty ourselves in faithful surrender and accept the promise, "*He shall be in you,*" then the Father will delight to fulfill it in our experience. We will then know that the beginning, and the secret, and the power of the life of a true disciple is in the indwelling Spirit.

PRAYER:

"Lord Jesus! My soul blesses you for your precious word, 'The Spirit shall be in you.' In deep humility I now once again accept it, and ask you to teach me its full meaning.

"I ask for myself, and for all believers everywhere, that we may see how near your love would come to us, and how entirely and most intimately you would give yourself to us. Nothing can satisfy you but to have your dwelling place within us, to abide in us as the life of our life. To this end you have sent forth, from your glory, the Holy Spirit into our hearts, to be the power that lives and acts in our innermost being, and to give within us the revelation of yourself, the glorified Jesus.

"O Lord Jesus, bring your Church to see this revelation that has been hidden and lost, that we would experience it, and bear witness to it in power. May the joyful sound be heard throughout, that every true believer has the indwelling and

the leading of your Spirit. And teach me the life of faith that waits on you, as your Spirit does your work within me. May my life continuously be in the holy and humble consciousness that Christ's Spirit dwells in me. I bow before this holy mystery. My Lord Jesus! Your own Spirit dwells in me! Amen"

CHAPTER 7

THE SPIRIT GIVEN TO THE OBEDIENT

"If you love me, keep My commandments; and I will pray the Father, and He will give you another Helper... the Spirit of Truth." John 14:15, 16

The Holy Spirit, whom God has given to those that obey Him. Acts 5:32

The truth of these words has often suggested the question: How can this be? Don't we need the Spirit to even *make* us obedient so we can *be* obedient? We long for the Spirit's power because we are so powerless over the disobedience within us, and we desire to be changed. But now Jesus claims obedience as the condition of the Father's giving, and our receiving the Spirit. What are we to do?

Let us first remember that there are two manifestation of the Spirit of God, corresponding to the old and the new testaments.

In the former he works as the Spirit of God, *preparing* the way for the higher revelation of God as the Father of Jesus Christ. He also worked in this manner in Christ's disciples, as the Spirit of conversion and faith. What they were now about to receive was something higher, a second manifestation, the Spirit of the glorified Jesus, communicating the power and the experience of his full salvation to them.

In the new covenant, while all believers have the Spirit in them as the Spirit of Christ, there is still something more to be received. Where there is little knowledge of the Spirit's purpose and work, the evidence of his presence in a church or individual is weak. Believers there will not get beyond the experience of his initial work of redemption; though he is in them, they do not know him in his power as the Spirit of the glorified Jesus. They have him in them to make them obedient. And only as they *are* obedient will they be promoted to the higher experience of his conscious indwelling, the representative and revealer of Jesus in his glory. *"If you love me, keep my commandments; and I will pray the Father, and He will send you another Helper."*

This is a lesson we cannot study enough. In the heavenly realm, even in Jesus, his close experience of the Father, his life, and his love, could only be met through obedience. God's revealed will is the expression of his hidden perfection and nature. As we give up our will to accept and do his will, to be possessed and used as he pleases, we are made ready by the Holy Spirit to enter his presence. This was Jesus's experience too. It was after he spoke his words of consecration, *"It is fitting for us to fulfill all righteousness,"* (Matthew 3:15), and gave himself in humility and obedience in baptism for the sins of the people, that he was then baptized with the Holy Spirit and power. The Spirit came because of his obedience. Later, after he had learned obedience in suffering, and became obedient even to death on the cross, he again received the Spirit from the Father, (see Acts 2:33), to pour out upon his disciples. The fullness of the Spirit for his body of believers was the reward for his obedience. This principle of the Spirit's coming is true for every member of his body - even as it was revealed in Jesus - that obedience is the essential key and condition of the Spirit's indwelling. *"If you love me, keep my commandments; and the Father will send you the Spirit."* Jesus came to prepare the way for the Spirit's coming. His outward coming in the flesh, was the preparation of his inward coming in the Spirit, to fulfill the promise of God in us. The Lord's outward coming appealed and affected the people in their soul, with its mind and feelings. It was only as Christ in his outward coming was accepted, loved and obeyed, that the inward and more intimate revelation would be given. And it was as his disciples grew close to him and accepted him as their Lord and master, and were willing to obey him, that they were made ready for the baptism of the Holy Spirit. It is the same with us; as we are faithful to listen to our conscience and keep his commands, and we prove our love to him, our hearts will be prepared for the fullness of the Spirit. We may fall short of this, and be forced to admit that what we want to do we cannot do. But if he sees the willingness of our surrender, and our obedience to the leadings of the Spirit that we have received so far, we may be certain that the fullness of the Spirit won't be withheld.

Don't these words suggest the reasons why the Church today is so limited in its experience of the presence and power of the Holy Spirit? We do not understand that as obedience must precede the fullness of the Spirit, so we must also *wait* for the fullness to follow. Those who want the fullness before obedience, stumble just the same as those who think their obedience is proof that they already have the fullness.

Obedience must precede the baptism of the Holy Spirit. John preached that Jesus was the true baptizer, who would baptize with the Holy Spirit and fire. Jesus took his disciples into a three year training course to make them ready. He instructed them personally, teaching them to forsake everything for him. He called himself their master and Lord, and taught them to do what he said. And then in his final words before the cross, he spoke repeatedly of obedience to his commands as the one condition of all further spiritual blessing. I don't believe that the Church today has given this word *obedience* the same prominence that Christ gave it.

Perhaps this is due to our self-righteousness, super-grace, lack of repentance, and our absence of holiness. While the freedom of grace and the simplicity of faith has been preached, we have not emphasized the absolute necessity of obedience and holiness. It has been thought that only those who had the fullness of the Spirit could be obedient. It was not seen that obedience must precede the baptism of the Holy Spirit. Christ in us is the presence of God that the obedient will inherit; his indwelling life works in us and through us. It has not been understood that the gateway to the fullness of the Spirit, and the abiding presence of the Lord, is to obey the conscience and the words of Jesus, to have a walk that is worthy of the Lord.

Due to the neglect of this first truth, the second was also forgotten - *the obedient may expect the fullness of the Spirit.* The promise of the special, conscious, and active indwelling of the Holy Spirit to the obedient is not known by many believers today. The greater part of their life is spent in mourning over their own disobedience - or over their inability, or powerlessness to obey - instead of utilizing the strength of the Spirit already in them unto obedience. They have known about the Holy Spirit as being for those who are obedient, to give them the presence and reality of Jesus, that he can work in them even greater works than he did. Jesus lived an outward life of trials and obedience in preparation for the hidden life of power and glory! It is in this inner life that we are made partakers of the gift of the Spirit of the glorified Jesus. But in our inner personal participation with that gift, we must walk in the way he prepared for us. It is only in the crucifixion of the flesh, do we yield ourselves to God's will - for him to do in us what he wills - and for us to know and do his perfect will. God will be known and found only in his will; his will is in Christ, and the heart which has become the home of the Holy Spirit. The perfect obedience of the Son was the condition for his receiving and giving the Holy Spirit. And the acceptance of the Son in love and obedience is the way to receive the indwelling of the Spirit.

This truth has come home powerfully to the hearts of many through the use of words such as *full surrender,* and *entire consecration.*

As they understood the absolute necessity of surrender and obedience, they found through grace, the entrance to a life of peace and strength previously unknown. Many are learning, or need to learn, that they still do not fully know this lesson. They will find that there are still applications of this principle beyond what we have mentioned. As we possess the Holy Spirit and he possess us, his presence in our life and our work will exceed anything we could ever ask and think. The indwelling of the Spirit was intended by God to be so much more than we have yet known! Let us yield ourselves to him in love and obedience so that our hearts may be enlarged and prepared for his fullness.

Let us pray to God that he would wake up his Church and his people to take in the simplicity of this lesson - *1.) **Obedience is necessary to receive the full experience of the Spirit's indwelling, 2.) The full experience of the Spirit's indwelling is what obedience may claim.*** Let each of us confess to the Lord that we love hm and that we will keep his commands. However weak we feel, or how often we have failed, speak this to him as the one purpose of our souls. He will accept it! In faith let us believe that the full indwelling of the Spirit, with the revelation of Christ within us, is ours. And let us be content with nothing less than the conscious thought that we are the Temples of the Living God, because the Spirit of God dwells in us.

PRAYER:

"Blessed Lord Jesus! With my whole heart I accept your teaching. And I ask you to write this truth ever deeper in my heart as one of the laws of your kingdom, that loving obedience may expect loving acceptance, sealed by an ever increasing experience of the power of the Spirit.

"I thank you for what your word teaches of the love and obedience of your disciples; though they were still imperfect, yet you covered them with your love. 'The spirit is willing, but the flesh is weak'. Lord Jesus, with my whole heart I say I do love you and desire to keep each of your commands.

41

"To every reproof of my conscience, I bow very low. To every moving of your Spirit, I yield in implicit obedience. Into your death I will give my will and life, that being raised with you, the life of your Holy Spirit now dwells in me, and reveals you to me, and he is now my life. Amen."

CHAPTER 8

KNOWING THE SPIRIT

"The Spirit of Truth, whom the world cannot receive, because it neither sees Him nor knows Him; but you know Him, for He dwells with you and will be in you." John 14:17

Do you not know that you are the Temple of God and that the Spirit of God dwells in you? 1 Corinthians 3:16

The value of true knowledge in the life of faith cannot be emphasized enough. If someone has been awarded an inheritance, yet they don't know about it, or they find a treasure, but don't know how to retrieve it, in both situations they're not any richer because they did not possess them. In the same way the gifts of God cannot be utilized properly until we know about them and possess them. In Christ are hidden all the treasures of wisdom and knowledge. It is for the treasure of Christ *himself* that the believer is willing to count everything else as loss. And it is because of the lack of the true knowledge of what God has prepared for us in Christ, that the lives of many believers are weak and without purpose. Paul's prayer in the book of Ephesians - that the Father would give them the Spirit of wisdom and revelation in the knowledge of him, that the eyes of their heart would be enlightened, (or opened), that they might know the hope of their calling and the riches of their inheritance, and the exceeding greatness of the power working within them, (see Ephesians 1:17-19) - is one we can never pray enough, whether for ourselves or for others. But it is especially important that we should know the teacher through whom all other knowledge is to come! The Father has given each one of his children, not only Christ, who is the truth, but also the Holy Spirit, *who is the very Spirit of Christ, and the Spirit of truth.* We received the Spirit who is *from God,* that we might know the things which are freely given to us *by God.*

Here is an important question: how do we know when it is the Spirit that is teaching us? In order for us to be certain in our knowledge of the things of God, we must know the teacher personally. It is only in knowing him who is truth, that we can be confident that our spiritual knowledge is also true. The Lord Jesus responds to this serious question by assuring us that we will actually know the Holy Spirit. When a messenger comes to speak to a king, or when a witness gives a testimony for his friend, neither speaks of himself. And yet, without intending to, as they both speak, they draw attention to themselves and their trustworthiness. In the same way, the Holy Spirit must be known and acknowledged when he testifies of Christ and glorifies him. This is the only way that we can have the assurance that the knowledge we receive is from God, and not what our human understanding has come up with from the bible. To know the king's seal is the only safeguard against a counterfeit image; to know the Spirit is the godly assurance of being certain.

How can we know the Spirit like this? Jesus says, "*You know Him, for He abides with you, and shall be in you.*" The abiding indwelling of the Spirit is the condition of knowing him; his presence will be self-evident. As we allow him to dwell in us, to take possession of our lives, and to testify of Jesus as Lord, he will bring his own credentials. He will prove himself to be the Spirit of God. *It is the Spirit that bears witness, because the Spirit is truth.* Because the presence of the Spirit as the indwelling teacher in each believer is so little known and recognized today, the workings of the Spirit are few and weak, and there is much hesitation and fear in acknowledging the witness of the Spirit. As the truth and experience of the indwelling Spirit is restored among God's people, and the Spirit is free again to work in power among us, his presence will be his own proof - we will indeed know him. *"You know Him, for He shall be in you."*

Meanwhile, since he is so little recognized, and his workings are so limited, how is he to be known? The answer is very simple - if you honestly want to know that you have the Spirit, and to know him as your personal possession and teacher, study the teachings of the word of God regarding the Spirit. Don't be content with the teachings of men or the Church about the Spirit, go directly to the word of God. And don't be content with your ordinary reading of the word, or what you think you already know of its doctrines. If you sincerely want to know the Spirit, then search as one thirsting to drink deeply of the water of life. Gather together everything that the bible says about the Holy Spirit and his indwelling, and hide it in your heart. Be determined to accept nothing less than what the word teaches - but also be determined to accept *all that it teaches.*

Study the word in complete dependence upon the Spirit's teaching. If you study it with your human wisdom and understanding, you may only confirm your already mistaken viewpoints. If you are a child of God you already have the Holy Spirit to teach you, even though you may not yet know how he works in you. Ask the Father to work through him in you, to make the word become your life and light. If you humbly submit yourself to the word of God and trust in his guidance, the promise will be fulfilled and you will be taught by God himself. We have spoken previously of the progress from the outward to the inward; be wholehearted in giving up all your thoughts, and the thoughts of men as you accept God's word. Ask him to reveal in you by his Spirit his own thoughts concerning his Spirit. He will do it!

And what will be the primary marks found in the word by which the Spirit in us can be known? There will be two - the *first* will be more external, referring to the work he does, and the *second* will be more internal, in the inner life, in the dispositions which he seeks in those whom he dwells.

We saw previously how Jesus spoke of obedience as the condition of the Spirit's coming, and his presence. Jesus gave him to us as our teacher and guide. All of scripture speaks of his work as demanding the surrender of our entire life. *If by the Spirit you put to death the deeds of the body, you shall live; for as many as are led by the Spirit of God, these are the sons of God.* (Romans 8:13, 14). *Your body is a temple of the Holy Spirit; glorify God therefore in your body.* (1 Corinthians 6:19, 20). *If we live in the Spirit, let us also walk in the Spirit.* (Galatians 5:25). *We are changed into the same image, even as by the Spirit of the Lord.* (2 Corinthians 3:18). These words clearly define the operations of the Spirit. As God is first known in his works, so it is with the Spirit; he reveals God's will and Christ doing his will, and calls us to follow him in it. As the believer surrenders himself and willingly consents to the life and the leading of the Spirit in the putting to death of the flesh, in obedience to Christ, and as he waits on the Spirit to work all this out in him, he will discover the wonder that the Spirit *is* working in him. If we make the aim of the Holy Spirit our aim, and give ourselves up entirely to him, then we'll be prepared to know him as dwelling in us. As we are led by him to obey God, even as Christ did, it will be the Spirit himself bearing witness with our spirit that he dwells in us.

We will know him better and more intimately as we yield ourselves to the life he works in us, and also as we study how the personal relationship that a believer has with him may be fully experienced. The primary characteristic of the soul that the Spirit desires to dwell in us is summed up in one word - *faith*. Faith has to do with the invisible, with what appears to man most unlikely. When the divine appeared in Jesus, it came hidden in an infant! For thirty years he lived in Nazareth, and they saw nothing in him but the son of a carpenter. It was only with his baptism that his divine Sonship came into complete and perfect view. Even to his disciples his divine glory was often hidden. How much more so, when the life of God enters the depths of our sinful being, will it require *faith* to recognize it? Let us meet the Spirit in holy and humble faith. Let us not be content to just know that he is in us - that profits us very little. Let us cultivate the habit of bowing before God in all things and give the Spirit the recognition that is due him. Let us wait on the Spirit in deep dependence on him, setting aside the flesh that is so willing to serve. As we enter the inner temple of our hearts in full surrender to the Spirit, we then bow to the Father and receive in faith the fullness of the Holy Spirit. Regardless of how little we see or feel, by faith let us believe. The divine is always first known by believing. As we continue to believe we will be prepared to know and see.

There is no way of knowing a fruit except by tasting it. There's no way of knowing the light other than being in the light and using it. There's no way of knowing a person except by interacting with him or her. And there is no way of knowing the Holy Spirit except by possessing him, and being possessed by him. To live in the Spirit is the only way to know the Spirit. To have him in us, doing his work and giving us his fellowship, and guiding our whole life, is the path the Lord Jesus opened when he said, *"You know Him, for He shall be in you."*

Believer, it was for the excellency of the knowledge of Jesus Christ that the apostle Paul counted all things as loss. Shouldn't we do the same? Shouldn't we be willing to give up everything in order to know the glorified Christ through the Holy Spirit? Think on that! The Father sent the Spirit for the sole purpose that we might fully share in the glory of the risen Christ! Shall we not give ourselves up completely to have him in us, that we may fully know him, through whom alone we can know the Son and the Father? Let us yield ourselves fully to the complete indwelling and teaching of the blessed Holy Spirit, whom the Son has given us from the Father.

PRAYER:

"Father, in the name of Jesus, you sent us your Holy Spirit. I pray that I may know him by having him within me. May his witness to me of Jesus be divinely clear and powerful. May his leading and sanctifying be in such holy power, and may his indwelling in my spirit be in such truth and life, that the consciousness of him as my life may be as simple and sure as my natural life. As the light is the sufficient witness to the sun, may his light be its own witness to the presence of Christ.

"Lead me, Father, in knowing him, to know correctly the mystery of your life in giving him to me to dwell within. The Holy Spirit was sent to us so that your personal presence, our unbroken and intimate union, might be my portion. Holy Spirit, your very life and self has now come to be the life of my life. Please take me wholly for your own.

"Father, teach me, and all of your people, to know your Spirit. Not only to know that he is in us, or somewhat of his workings, but to know him as in his very person he reveals and glorifies the Son, and the Son reveals and glorifies you, our Father. Glory to God in the highest! Thank you, and Amen."

CHAPTER 9

THE SPIRIT OF TRUTH

"But when the Helper comes, whom I shall send to you from the Father, the Spirit of Truth who proceeds from the Father, He will testify of Me." John 15:26

"When He, the Spirit of Truth has come, He will guide you into all truth for He will not speak from His own authority; but whatever He hears He will speak." John 16:13

God created man in his own image to become like himself, capable of having true fellowship with him in his glory. In Paradise there were two ways set before man for reaching this likeness of God, symbolized by the two trees - one of life, and the other of knowledge. God's way was life - only through life would man come to the knowledge and likeness of God. By abiding in God's will and participating in God's life, man would be perfected. However, Satan convinced man that possessing knowledge, more than giving obedience, was the main thing to be pursued to make us like God. And when man chose the *light of knowledge* above the *life of obedience*, he stepped foot upon a terrible path that leads only to death. The desire to *know* became his greatest temptation. His whole nature became corrupted, and knowledge was more important to him than obedience and life.

Today the human race is still being led astray by the power of this deceitful promise of happiness through knowledge. And nowhere is its influence more terribly seen than in connection with Christianity, and God's own revelation of himself. Even where the word of God is accepted, the wisdom of the world and the flesh still enters in. Spiritual truth is robbed of its divine power when held in the wisdom of man, rather than in the life of the Spirit. When truth, as God desires it, enters into the inward parts of a man or a woman, it becomes the life of the Spirit. But if truth only reaches the outer parts of our soul, with its mind, intellect, and reason, it may occupy and satisfy in some way, but it is nothing more than human argument and wisdom. It never touches the true life of the Spirit. There is a natural truth of the understanding and feelings within human nature, which is a shadow of divine truth. And there is a truth which is substance and reality, communicating to the one who holds it, the actual possession and reality of the life of things which others can only think and speak. The natural truth in shadow, form, and thought, was all that the law could give - and that was all that the religion of the Jews consisted of. The truth of substance and a divine life was what Jesus brought to us as the Son of God, full of grace and truth. He is himself *the truth.*

In promising the Holy Spirit to his disciples, the Lord speaks of him as the *Spirit of Truth.* The truth, grace, and life that he brought from heaven to us as an extraordinary spiritual reality, exist only in the Spirit of God. He is the Spirit and the inner life of that divine truth. When we receive him and give ourselves up to him, he makes Christ and the life of God to be divinely understood truth in us. In his teaching and guiding into the truth, he does not simply give us thoughts or ideas as from a teacher or a book, but he enters the secret roots of our life and plants the truth of God there as a seed, and then dwells in it, and grows it within us as the divine life. As we surrender to him in faith and expectation, he stimulates and nourishes our hidden life, and it is strengthened and spreads its influence throughout our entire being. So, it is not from without, but from within, not in words, but in power, and in life and truth that the Spirit reveals Christ and all he has for us. He makes Christ - who may have been only a savior, an image, a thought, or God outside of us, somewhere 'up there' - to be truth within us. The Spirit brings with his incoming the truth into us, and then possessing us he guides us from within into all of it.

When he promised to send the Spirit of truth from the Father, the Lord Jesus declared that his principle work would be, *"He shall bear witness of Me."* He spoke this just moments before he proclaimed, *"I am the truth."* The Spirit of truth has no other work than to reveal and impart the fullness of grace and truth that lives in Christ. He came to bear witness in us and through us, of the reality of the glory and power that Christ's redemption has accomplished. There are many who fear that thinking too much about the Spirit's presence within us will lead us away from Christ. This may be true if we're looking only at ourselves, but we can be sure that as we recognize him within us, he will lead us to a deeper and fuller understanding of Christ himself as our fullness and life. *"He shall bear witness of Me - He shall glorify Me."* It is he who will make our knowledge of Christ's life and truth an experience of the power with which he works and saves.

The Lord Jesus uses some amazing language concerning the Spirit. *"He will guide you into all Truth, for He will not speak from Himself, but whatever He hears He will speak,"* John 16:13. The mark of the Spirit of truth within us is a wonderful godly teachableness. In the mystery of the three-in-one God, there is nothing more beautiful than this - there is a divine equality between the Son and the Spirit, and perfect submission. The Son could have claimed that men should honor him even as they honored the Father, yet he did not count it as a loss of honor to say, *"The Son can do nothing of Himself, for as I hear, so I speak,"* (see John 5:19). Likewise the Spirit of truth never speaks from his own self - because he is

God he could, but he does not. He only speaks what he hears. The Spirit of truth is the Spirit that fears to speak out of its own - it only speaks when, and what God speaks.

This is the disposition he works, and the life he breathes into those who truly receive him. The gentle teachableness which marks the poor in spirit and the broken in heart, who take no thought of their own wisdom or righteousness, but only seek Christ as their life, are the ones that the Spirit within them can be the Spirit of truth. He exposes us as we handle the word of God, showing us that we lack a humble and submissive spirit, which prevents us from discovering its true spiritual meaning. He opens our eyes as to why so much bible reading, study, and preaching bears so little of the fruit of holiness. It is because it is studied and held with a wisdom that is not waited for, or acquired from God - the Spirit of truth is not present. He does not speak and does not think from himself - he only speaks what he hears. The Spirit of truth receives everything day by day, and step by step from God in heaven. He is silent and does not speak, except, and when, he hears.

There is a great danger in the Christian life - seeking to know the truth of God in his word without waiting on the Spirit of truth within the heart. The enemy of mankind still moves about among men, and knowledge is still his great means of temptation. There are many Christians today who would profess that their knowledge of divine truth does very little for them - it leaves them empty and powerless against the world and sin. They know very little of the light and the liberty, as well as the strength and the joy, that truth is meant to bring. It is because they seek God's truth in the power of human thought and wisdom, and not the Spirit of truth. Most of our earnest efforts to abide in Christ, and to walk like him, have failed because our faith stood more in the wisdom of men, rather than the power of God. Most of our experiences have been short lived because they did not utilize the Spirit of truth, who was within us to make Christ and his holy presence a living reality.

Jesus said, *"If any man will come after Me, let him deny himself... and follow Me,"* (see Matthew 16:24; Mark 8:34; Luke 9:23). Many have attempted to follow him without denying themselves. There is nothing that needs to be denied more than the energy and wisdom of our natural mind, as it inserts itself into the things of God. We must acknowledge that apart from the Holy Spirit leading us, we cannot pray, or study, or worship, or serve - in our own ability and wisdom we can do nothing. We need to deny - perhaps even more than our own righteousness - our own wisdom. This is often the most difficult part of the denial of self. In our worship we need to realize the all-sufficiency and vital importance, not only of the blood, but also the Spirit of Christ. This is the meaning of the call to be silent before God and wait on him, to silence the rush of thoughts and words in God's presence, and in deep humility and stillness, to simply wait and listen to what God will say. The Spirit of truth never speaks from himself - what he hears he then speaks. A listening and teachable spirit is the evidence of the presence of the Spirit of truth.

When we wait, let us remember that the Spirit of truth may not speak to us initially in thoughts or words that we can understand. The Holy Spirit is the Spirit of truth because he is the Spirit of Life, and the life is the light of men. He does not speak initially to our thoughts or feelings, but in the hidden places of the heart, to the spirit of a man or a woman, in their inmost parts. It is only by faith that the meaning and the truth of his teaching is revealed. Therefore, let our first work be to believe and trust the Living God in the work he undertakes to do. Let us believe in the Holy Spirit as the divine giver of life, and the one who sanctifies - who is already within us - and let us yield and surrender everything to him. He will prove himself to be the divine enlightener - his life is the light. Let our confession that we have no life- or goodness of our own - be joined with the confession that we have no wisdom either. The deeper our sense of this, the greater the realization of the Spirit's guidance will become. As the Spirit works more within us to bring us into the likeness of God, and as we continue to trust and abide in him, he will reveal the secrets of the Lord. He is the Spirit of truth.

PRAYER:

"Oh God of truth! In those that worship you, you seek truth in the inward parts. I bless you again that you have given me the Spirit of Truth, and that he now dwells in me. I pray that I may know him rightly, and walk before you in full consciousness that the Spirit of Truth, which is the Spirit of Christ, is indeed within the inmost parts of my new life. May my every thought and word, my every disposition and habit, be the proof that the Spirit of Christ, who is the truth, lives and rules within me.

"I especially ask you that he may witness to me of Christ Jesus. May the truth of his atonement and blood dwell in me, and I in it. May his life and glory be truth in me, a living experience of his presence and power. Father, may the Spirit of your Son, the Spirit of Truth, indeed be my life. May each word of the Lord Jesus Christ through the Holy Spirit be made truth in me.

"Father, I thank you once again that he dwells within me. I ask that you would grant, according to the riches of your glory, that he may work mightily in me and all your saints. Oh, that all your people may know this is their privilege and rejoice in it - the Holy Spirit, who is the Spirit of Truth, lives within them to reveal Christ, who is truth in them. Amen."

CHAPTER 10

THE EXPEDIENCY OF
THE SPIRIT'S COMING

*"I tell you the truth. It is to your advantage that I go away:
for if I do not go away, the Helper will not come to you; but
if I depart, I will send Him to you." John 16:7*

As the Lord was leaving this world, he made a promise
to his disciples that his leaving would be in their best
interest; he was going to send the Helper to come and
take his place, who would be closer and more effective to them
than he, himself, had ever been in his physical presence. This is
very special for a couple of reasons: his fellowship with them had
never been broken, but now it would be completely broken off by
death and they would never see him again; however, the Helper,
the Holy Spirit, would now abide with them forever. His own
relationship with them had been external, and it had not produced
what we might have expected, but the Spirit would be *in* them;

his coming would be as an indwelling presence, with the power of Jesus Christ himself in them as their life and strength.

During his life on earth, Jesus interacted with each of his disciples according to their unique character and circumstances. His fellowship with each one was personal and thoughtful, with the wisdom to meet their individual needs. Would the Holy Spirit be able to supply this need to them as well, giving them the individual attention and love, which made Jesus so precious? Yes, indeed! All the blessings that the Lord Jesus had been to them, the Spirit was about to bring back in an even greater power and experience, to be with them forever. They would be far happier, safer, and stronger with Jesus in heaven than they could have ever been with him on earth. The primary quality of their life with Jesus was his thoughtful and caring friendship - the indwelling of the Holy Spirit was meant to restore his most personal fellowship, communion and guidance, *and* his close and intimate friendship.

This idea may be hard for many to grasp or believe, and even more difficult to experience. The thought of Jesus walking and living, and guiding us on earth is very clear. But the concept of him hiding himself within us, and instead of speaking to us directly, would speak to us in the secret recesses of our heart, makes his guidance seemingly even more difficult to understand. And yet the very things which make this so difficult to conceive is what gives it its greater worth and glory. This principle is true in daily life, where difficulty strengthens the will and develops character, and brings about maturity. In a child's first lessons he has to be helped and encouraged; as he goes on to what is more difficult, the teacher leaves him to his own resources; finally the youth leaves his parent's home to have the principles that have been instilled in him tested and strengthened. And in us, it is expedient that the outward presence and help be withdrawn, that the internal lessons that we have been taught can be applied to our whole being.

God wants to bring us into a mature perfection, not ruled by an outward law, but by the inner life. As long as Jesus was with the disciples on the earth, he worked from the outside in, and yet he could never effectively reach or master their inner life. But when he went away he sent the Spirit to be in them, that their growth might now come from the inside out. By first taking possession of them through his Spirit in the secret places of their inner man, he would have them surrender and consent to his life and leading - he would be in them. They would then have the guidance and framing of their life, and the forming of their character within them, through the power of the Holy Spirit, who had become their spirit. They would then grow up confident and independent from outward influences, becoming like the Lord Jesus himself, a true and separate person, having life in himself, yet living in full dependance on the Father.

As long as we only ask for what is easy and pleasant, we'll never understand that it is expedient, and actually better for us, that Christ *should not* be physically on the earth. If we would set aside our inconvenience, and consider the possibility that we could actually become like Jesus, and be changed into his image and likeness, then the idea of his leaving so that the Spirit can come and be our very own teacher and guide would seem wonderful and amazing. However, this may be a much more difficult and dangerous path than it would have been to follow him on the earth. But keep in mind that the divine life and nobility that we are gaining through this new level of intimacy and fellowship with God in the Spirit is totally worth it. To have the Holy Spirit coming through the glorified human nature of Jesus, entering into our spirits, identifying himself with us, and becoming our very own, just as he was the Spirit of the Lord on the earth, is a blessing worth any sacrifice. *It is the beginning of the indwelling of God himself.*

However, to see it and desire it does not remove its degree of difficulty. How can the tender, special, and personal relationship of love that Jesus had for each of his disciples now be ours to the same degree with him absent, and the Spirit taking his place? The answer is *by faith*. When the disciples believed and walked with Jesus on the earth, they walked by sight, but now we walk by faith. It is by faith that we accept and rejoice in his words, *"It is to your advantage that I go away."* We must take the time to believe it and approve it, and then rejoice and give thanks that he has gone to the

Father, and that he has called us to participate in his life through the Spirit. Through faith we must believe that in his gift of the Holy Spirit we have full communion with his presence and life. It may come in ways we do not understand, but as we continue in faith and believe that his indestructible gift is true, and is in us, he will show us that our life with him is real, and is to be enjoyed.

"Will teach us." Beware of thinking that teaching means thoughts. We want the Spirit to suggest to us certain concepts of how Jesus will be with us and in us, but that's not what he does. The Spirit does not dwell in the mind, but in the *life*. It's not in what we know - or any truth, for that matter - in the beginning. Knowledge, thoughts, feelings, and actions are all part of the external influence which the physical presence of Jesus had upon the disciples. But the Spirit came, and went *in* them, deeper than all these. He was to be the hidden presence of Jesus *within* the depths of their personality. His life came into them in power to become their life, and his teaching would begin, not in words or thoughts, *but in power*. It would work in them with the presence, and the faith, and the energy of the Lord himself taking charge of their entire lives and circumstances. Through the Spirit they would know that by faith the risen Jesus now lives in them. And their faith, *which is his faith,* would be at once the cause and effect of the presence of the Lord in the Spirit.

This is the breath of faith which the Spirit gives us, that the life, nearness, and presence of Jesus will be as real to us as it was when he was on the earth. Why then don't believers who have the Spirit experience him more consciously and fully? The answer is they do not fully know and honor the Spirit who is *in* them. *They have much faith in the Christ who died, and who reigns in heaven, but they have little faith in Christ who dwells in them by his Spirit.* This is the faith we need, faith in Jesus as the one who fulfills the promise, *"He that believes in me, rivers of living water shall flow out of him."* We must believe this not only with the faith of our understanding of this truth, but also with our hearts, where the Holy Spirit dwells. The gift of the Holy Spirit and the entire teaching of Jesus concerning him, is to enforce the words, *"The kingdom of God is within you,"* (see Luke 17:20-21). If we desire this truth within us, then we must turn inward, and yield ourselves completely to the Spirit to do his work in us.

If we want this teaching and faith, which dwells in the life and power of the Holy Spirit, then above all let us fear what hinders him most - our own will and wisdom. Our flesh and the self life remains our greatest enemy. Even in our service to God, and in our efforts to exercise faith, the self life is constantly putting itself forward. Every thought and every effort, regardless if they are good or evil, must be brought into the captivity and obedience to Jesus Christ through the Spirit. (See 2 Corinthians 10:3-5). Let us cast our will and our own wisdom at the feet of Jesus, and wait for him there in faith and stillness. A deep consciousness of the life of the Spirit will begin to grow and manifest itself within us. When we honor him and give ourselves up fully to him, he will not shame us, but he will do his great work within us, as he strengthens our inner life, builds up our faith, and reveals the person of Jesus to us. And we will experience his presence and guidance in sweet communion as clearly and dearly as if he were with us in his physical body.

PRAYER:

"Blessed Lord Jesus, I rejoice that you are no longer physically here on the earth. I bless you that in a fellowship and communion more near, more tender, and more effective than if you were still here, you now manifest yourself to us. I thank you that your Holy Spirit dwells within me, and helps me to know what that fellowship is, and what is the reality of your holy indwelling.

"Lord, forgive me that I have not truly known your Spirit sooner or better, and that I have not praised and loved you rightly for this most wonderful gift of the Father's love. Teach me, by faith, to believe in you more completely, from whom the fresh anointing flows and fills the life daily.

"Oh Lord, I cry to you on behalf of so many of your redeemed ones, who do not yet see what it is to give up and

lose the mixed life after the flesh, and to receive in its place the life that is the power of the Spirit. Along with many of your saints, I pray that you would please grant that the Church may be awakened to know how the one mark of her calling, the one secret of her enjoyment of your presence, the one power for fulfilling her assignment, is that each believer would be led to know that the Spirit dwells with him, and that the abiding presence of his Lord with him as keeper and guide and friend, is indeed his sure portion. Grant this, Lord Jesus, for your glory and honor. Amen."

CHAPTER 11

THE SPIRIT
GLORIFYING JESUS

"It is to your advantage that I go away; for if I do not go away, the Helper will not come to you; but if I depart, I will send Him to you... He will glorify Me, for He will take of what is Mine and declare it to you." John 16:7,14

Scripture speaks of two ways in which the Son is glorified - one is by the Father, and the other by the Holy Spirit; one takes place in heaven, and the other here on earth. By the first, he is glorified *in God Himself* - by the second, he is glorified *in us,* (see John 13:32; 17:10). Of the first, Jesus said, *"If God is glorified in Him, (the Son of Man), God will also glorify Him in Himself, and glorify Him immediately."* (John 13:32). And again, in the high priestly prayer, *"Father, the hour has come. Glorify Your Son... and now, Father, glorify Me together with Yourself,"* (see John 17:1, 5). Of the second, he said, *"The Spirit shall glorify me. I am glorified in them."*

To glorify is to manifest and reveal the hidden excellence and worth of an object. Jesus, as the Son of Man, was glorified when his human nature was fully brought into the power and glory of the Father. He entered into the perfect spirit life of heaven and God himself. And all the angels worshipped him as the Lamb who sits on the throne. This heavenly spiritual glory of Christ is one the human mind cannot quite understand. It can only be truly communicated through the Spirit as it is experienced, known, and received in the inner life. This is the work of the Holy Spirit, as the Spirit of the glorified Christ. Coming down to us as the Spirit of glory, he reveals the glory of Christ in us, with the same life and power of the glory that Christ has. He makes Christ glorious to us, in us, and through us to those who have eyes to see. (See John 3:3). The Son does not seek his own glory - the Father glorifies him in heaven, and the Spirit glorifies him *in us.*

But for Christ to be glorified by the Spirit, he needed to first leave his disciples. They could not have him in the flesh and in the Spirit at the same time; his physical presence would hinder the Spirit's indwelling. They had to part with the Christ they had, before they could receive the Christ to come - the glorified Christ through the Holy Spirit. And Jesus Christ himself had to give up the life he had on earth before he could be glorified in heaven, and then in us. Even in our union with him, we have to let go of the Christ we think we know, and the limited measure of the life we may have with him, if we are to have him fully glorified to us, in us, and through us by the Holy Spirit.

I am convinced that many believers do not fully understand the Lord when he says, *"It is to your advantage that I go away."* Like his own disciples, they have believed in him, loved him, obeyed him, and they have experienced much of the great blessing of knowing and following him. And yet they feel that there is still something missing. They have yet to experience the deep rest and joy, the holy light, and the divine power of his abiding within them that is described in the scriptures. They have yet to fully inherit the promise, *"The Helper shall abide with you, and he shall be in you. He shall glorify Me."* They can't grasp the great advantage they will have in Christ's leaving them, so that he might come again glorified in the Spirit. And they are not yet able to say, *Even though we have known Christ according to the flesh, yet now we know him thus no longer,* (see 2 Corinthians 5:16).

The only way to accomplish this is to end our *knowing Christ according to the flesh.* We must make room for knowing him only in the power of the Spirit. *According to the flesh* means in the power of the external - of the words, thoughts, efforts, feelings, influences, or aids coming from men. The believer who has received the Holy Spirit, but who has not yet completely surrendered to his leading and indwelling, still has his understanding and confidence in the flesh. While admitting that he can do nothing without the Holy Spirit, he still vainly labors and struggles to believe and live as he knows he should. He may boldly confess that Christ alone is his life and strength, yet in secret he grieves at how often he fails in allowing Christ to live out his own life through him. He tries to believe that Christ is near, even within him, yet there always seems to be breaks and interruptions. It is as if faith is not what it should be, the substance of the things we had hoped for. The reason is that faith itself is still too much the work of the mind, the power of the flesh, and the wisdom of man. He has had a revelation of Christ, but that revelation has been taken over, at least in part, by the power of the flesh and the wisdom of his own mind. This has rendered the revelation of Christ powerless - the Christ of glory, and the doctrine of the indwelling Christ, has been received into the mixed life of part flesh and part spirit. It is only the Holy Spirit who can glorify Jesus Christ. We must give up and set aside our old ways of knowing, believing, and having Christ, no longer knowing him after the flesh. *"The Spirit shall glorify Me."*

What does it mean that the Spirit glorifies Christ? And what is this glory of Christ that he reveals, and how does he do it? We learn from the scriptures about his glory. It says in Hebrews, *We do not yet see all things made subject to man. But we see Jesus crowned with glory and honor,* (see Hebrews 2:8, 9). All things have been subjected to him. So the Lord connects his being glorified with all things being given to him. *"He shall glorify Me, for He shall receive what is Mine, and show it to you," (John 16:14, 15).* And as he said to the Father, *"All things that are Mine are Yours, and Yours are Mine; and I am glorified in them,"* (John 17:10). The Father exalted him above all rule, power, and dominion, and placed all things under his feet. He gave the glorified Christ the name which is above every name, that at the name of Jesus every knee should bow. The kingdom and the power and the glory are forever one - unto him who sits on the throne, and to the Lamb in the midst of the throne, be glory and dominion forever. It is as he sits on the throne of the divine glory, with all things put in subjection under his feet, (see Ephesians 1:20-22), that Jesus has been glorified in heaven.

When the Holy Spirit glorifies Jesus in us, he takes the things of the glorified Christ and declares them to us. It is not that he gives us a thought or vision of that glory, but rather he shows it to us as a personal experience and possession to be received in our innermost life. He reveals Christ as present in us. All the true and living knowledge we have of him is through the Spirit of God. God's growth in us, from a feeble infant to perfected maturity, comes from, and through, the Holy Spirit. It all may happen, as it did with his disciples, accompanied by much darkness and failure. But when the Holy Spirit reveals the glorified Lord, the throne of his glory is established in our hearts, and he rules over every enemy from within us. Every power is brought into subjection, every thought into captivity to the obedience of Christ. In our renewed nature there rises the song, *Glory to Him who sits on the Throne.* Though the confession holds true to the end, *In my flesh there dwells no good thing,* the presence of Christ as our ruler so fills our heart and life that he rules over all. Sin has no authority over us; *the law of the Spirit of the Life in Christ Jesus has made me free from the law of sin and death,* (Romans 8:2).

If this is the glorifying of Christ which the Spirit brings, it is easy to see the way that leads to it. The enthronement of the Lord Jesus in his glory can only take place in the heart which has promised complete obedience. By faith it believes that he will take his power and rule within us, placing every enemy under his feet. It yields everything to his Lordship, and gives him full possession of all things, through the Holy Spirit. It is only in the obedient disciple that the Spirit is promised to dwell, and there in him the Spirit glorifies Christ.

This only takes place where *the fullness of time* has come to the believing soul. The history of the Church, as a whole, tends to repeat itself in each individual believer. Until the time appointed by the Father comes, the heir is under guardians and stewards, and does not differ much from a servant. (See Galatians 4:1-2). But when the fullness of time has come, and faith has been perfected, the Spirit of the glorified Lord enters in power, and Christ dwells in the heart. Yes, the history of Christ himself repeats itself in the soul. In the temple there are two holy places, the one before the veil, called The Holy Place, and the other within the veil, called The Holiest of All. In his earthly life Christ dwelt and ministered in The Holy Place, outside the veil - the veil of his flesh kept him outside of The Holiest of All. It was only when the veil of the flesh was torn, and he died to sin completely and forever, that he could enter the innermost sanctuary of the full glory of the Spirit life in heaven.

Likewise the believer who longs to have Jesus glorified within him through the Spirit, regardless of how blessed his life has been in the knowledge and service of the Lord, must learn that there is something more. The veil of the flesh must be torn in him too; he must enter this special part of Christ's work through the new and living way into The Holiest of All. *He who has suffered in the flesh has ceased from sin,* (1 Peter 4:1). The soul must see how Jesus has completely triumphed over the flesh, and entered with it into the Spirit life, and that the Holy Spirit brings the power of the glorified Jesus to dwell in us, to remove the veil in us, and maintain our life before the Most Holy in the full presence of his glory.

The tearing of the veil and the enthronement of Jesus as the glorified one in the heart, is not always with the sound of trumpets and shouting. It may be that way for some, but in many it takes place deep within, with awe and trembling in stillness where not a sound is heard. Zion's king still comes in meekness and lowliness to bring his kingdom to the poor in spirit. Without any outward attractiveness he enters in, deeper down than thoughts and feelings, the Holy Spirit glorifies him to the faith that doesn't see, but still believes. The eyes of the flesh did not see him on the throne, and it was a mystery to the world. But when everything within seems weak and empty, rest assured that the Spirit is secretly working, and that Christ is being formed within, and he is taking up his residence. The soul now knows that Jesus is Lord and that his throne in the heart is established in righteousness. Now the promise is fulfilled, *"the Spirit shall glorify Me."*

PRAYER:

"Blessed Lord Jesus, I worship you in the glory which the Father has given you, and I bless you that the promise of that glory will be revealed in the hearts of your disciples, to dwell in them and fill them completely. This is your glory, that all that the Father has is now yours. You have said the Holy Spirit will take of what is yours and reveal it to us. Heaven and earth are full of your glory! May the hearts and lives of those who believe be filled with it too.

"Blessed be your name for all in whom the rich beginnings of the fulfillment has already come! Lord, let it go on from glory to glory. Teach us how to keep our separation unto you unbroken, that our heart and life shall be yours alone. Teach us to hold fast our confidence without wavering, that the Spirit who is within us will perfect his work. Above all, teach us to yield ourselves in ever increasing dependance and emptiness, to wait for the Spirit's teaching and leading. We desire to have no confidence in the flesh, or its wisdom, or its righteousness. I bow ever lower and deeper before you in the holy fear and reverence of the truth that your Spirit, the Holy Spirit, the Spirit of your glory, is within me to do his divine work. Blessed Lord, let him rise in great power and have full dominion within me and over me, that my heart may be fully made into the temple and the kingdom in which you alone are glorified, and in which your glory fills all in all. Amen."

CHAPTER 12

THE SPIRIT CONVICTING
OF SIN

"If I depart, I will send the Helper to you. And when He comes, He will convict the world of sin..." John 16:7-8

T he connection between the two statements in these words of scripture is not always noticed. Before the Holy Spirit would convict the world of sin, he would first come *into* the disciples. He would make his home and establish himself in them, and then from out of them, and through them, do his convicting work in the world. *"He shall bear witness of Me, and you shall also bear witness,"* (see John 15:26-27). The disciples would soon realize that the great work of the Holy Spirit, which is striving with man by convicting the world of sin, could only be done as he had a firm footing on the earth *in* them. They were to be baptized with the Holy Spirit and fire and receive the power from above, with the one purpose of being the instruments through whom the Holy Spirit would reach the world. The sin convicting power of the Spirit was to dwell in them and work through them. It was for this reason that the Lord Jesus sought to prepare them and us with the words above:

1.) The Holy Spirit came to us, that through us he may reach others. The Spirit is the Spirit of the Holy One, the redeeming God. When he enters us he does not change his nature, or lose his divine character, he is still the Spirit of God striving with man and seeking his deliverance. Wherever he is not hindered by ignorance or selfishness, he shines forth from the heart, his temple, for the work he has to do in the world. He makes us willing and bold to do that work, to testify against sin, and to testify for Jesus, the one who delivers from sin. He does this as the Spirit of the crucified and exalted Christ. What purpose was it that the Lord Jesus received the Spirit without measure? *"The Spirit of the Lord is upon Me, because He anointed Me to preach good tidings to the poor. He sent Me to proclaim release of the captives!"* (Luke 4:18). It was this same Spirit - through whom Christ had offered himself unto God, and through whom as the Spirit of Holiness, he had been raised from the dead - that he sent down to his Church. The Spirit was to have his home in them as he had in Christ. And in no lesser way than in Christ himself would the Holy Spirit in them pursue his work in men. As a light shining in the darkness, revealing, condemning and conquering as the Spirit of burning and judgment, he is to be to the world the power of divine conviction and conversion. Not from heaven as the Spirit of God, but from the hearts of men as the Holy Spirit, he would convict the world of sin. *"I will send Him to you, and when He comes, He will convict the world..."* It is *in* and *through* us that the Spirit can reach the world.

2.) The Spirit can only reach others through us by first bringing us into perfect harmony with himself. He enters us to become so *one* with us that he becomes the personality and life within us. Then his work in us and through us towards others becomes our work.

The application of this truth to the conviction of sin in the world is extremely serious. The words of the Lord Jesus are thought to be in reference to the continued conviction of sin which he will always be working within believers. In a sense this is true, this first work of the Spirit remains the significance of all his comforting and sanctifying work. It is only as he keeps alive the tender sense of the danger and shame of sin, that the soul will be kept in its low place before God, hiding in Jesus as its only safety and strength. As the Holy Spirit reveals and communicates the life of Christ within us, the sure result will be a deeper sense of the sinfulness of sin. But the words mean so much more. If the Spirit is to convict the world through us and our testimony, whether by our words or by our life, he must first convict *us* of sin. He must give each of us a deep sense of the guilt of its unbelief and its rejection of the Lord Jesus Christ. We must see and regard sin as he does, that it is the cause, and the proof, and the fruit of our rejection of him. There will then be an inner readiness for the Spirit to work through us, When there is a unity between our witness and his witness against sin for God, then there will be an inner readiness for the Spirit to work through us with his convicting power.

It is so easy to judge others in the power of the flesh, and not see the *"Get out of my way, I am holier than you"* spirit that flows out of us. We testify out of a wrong spirit, or from our own strength, or we're too weak and afraid to speak at all. It is because we see sin and the sinfulness of others out from our flesh, but not with the conviction that comes only from the Holy Spirit. When he convicts us of the sin of the world, his work bears two marks. The *first* is the sacrifice of self, in the jealousy for God and his honor, combined with a deep and tender grief for the guilty. The *second* is a deep and strong faith in the possibility and the power of deliverance. We see each sin in its terrible relation to the whole, and we see the whole in the light of the cross, and how sin is unspeakably hateful in its awful assault against God, and its fearful power over the poor soul. But we also see it as condemned, atoned for, put away and conquered in the Lord Jesus Christ. We learn to look upon the world as God sees it in his holiness, hating its sin with an infinite hatred, and yet loving it to the extent that he gave up his own Son. And the Son gave his life to destroy the world's sin and see its captives set free. May God give his people a true and deep conviction of the sin of the world in its rejection of Christ.

And may we be prepared by the Spirit to convict the world of its sin as we profess our belief in the Lord Jesus Christ.

3.) *The believer must pray for it, and bring their whole life under the leading of the Holy Spirit.* The various gifts of the Spirit all depend upon his personal indwelling and possession of the inner life, along with the revelation of Christ in us, who gave his life to have sin destroyed. When the Lord Jesus spoke that word of inexhaustible meaning, *"He shall be in you,"* he opened up the secret of all of the Spirit's teaching, sanctifying and strengthening. The Spirit is the life of Christ, and he enters in and the life of Christ becomes our life. As he influences and inspires us he will be able to work in us as he wills. The believer must become familiar with the different operations of the Spirit, that he loses nothing through neglect or ignorance. It is most important, with each new insight from the Spirit, to get a firmer hold of the truth. Let your life be in the Spirit, and his fullness will not be withheld. If you desire to have this profound spiritual conviction of the sin of the world, with the deep sense of its terrible power and exceeding sinfulness, and if you want to be equipped as one through whom the Spirit can convict sinners, then yield your whole life and being to the Holy Spirit. Let the thought of this wonderful mystery of the nearness and the indwelling of the Holy God in you quiet your mind and heart into beautiful fear and worship. Surrender the great enemy which opposes him - your flesh and the self life - everyday so that he will mortify it, and keep it dead. Be content with nothing less than being filled with the Spirit of Christ, whose glory is that he gave himself up unto death to take away sin, to bring our whole life and being under his inspiration and control. As your life in the Spirit becomes healthy and stronger, and as your spiritual foundation becomes energized, your eyes will see, and your heart will feel what the sin around you is. Your thoughts and feelings will be those of the Holy Spirit breathing in you. Your deep horror of sin, your rich faith in your redemption from it, your great love for the souls who are still in it, and your willingness to die like your Lord if they can be freed from it, will make you the right instrument for the Spirit to convict the world of its sin through you.

4.) He must dwell in us as the world's Convicter of sin. We are seeking in this book to find the way in which we can all be filled with the Holy Spirit. Here is one condition: *"I will send Him to you... and he will convict the world."* Offer yourself to him that you may consider, feel, and bear the sins of those around you. Let the sins of the world be your concern as much as your own sin. Don't their sins dishonor God as much as yours? Are they not equally provided for in the great redemption? Does not the Spirit dwelling in you long to convict them as well? The Holy Spirit dwelled in the body and the nature of Jesus, and was the source of all that he felt, said, and did; God worked out through him the will of his holy love. The Spirit now dwells in believers, to be the source of all they feel, say and do. The one purpose for the Christ, and now the Holy Spirit, was that sin might be conquered. This is the great objective for which the baptism of the Holy Spirit and fire was given: that in, and through believers he might convict the world of sin, and deliver them from it. Put yourself into contact with the world's sin. Meet it in the love and faith of the Lord Jesus Christ, as a servant and helper of the needy and hopeless. Give yourself to prove the reality of your faith in Christ by your likeness to him. Through you the Spirit will convict the world of its unbelief. Seek the full experience of the indwelling Spirit, not for your own selfish enjoyment, but for this one purpose, that he would do the Father's work *through you,* as he did through Jesus. Live in unity and love with other believers, working and praying that men may be saved out of sin - *then the world will believe that God has sent Him.* It is the life of believers living in self-sacrificing love that will prove to the world that Christ is a reality, and so convict it of its sin of unbelief.

The success with which a man lives and carries on his business depends much upon his having a suitable building for it. When the Holy Spirit comes into a surrendered life, fully given over to him as his home, he fills him with God's thoughts towards sin, and releases his power in him to work. There is no clearer way to receive the full measure of the Spirit than to be wholly yielded to him, to let the very mind of Christ in regard to sin work in us.

He took away sin by the sacrifice of himself through the Eternal Spirit. What the Spirit was in him, he seeks to be in us - what was true of him, must also be true in us.

If you want to be filled with the Holy Spirit, have a sure understanding of this - the Holy Spirit is in you to convict the world of sin. If you are fully identified with him in this, then you may be sure that he will dwell in you completely, and work in you powerfully. The primary objective for which Christ came was to put away sin; the primary work for which the Holy Spirit comes to men is to persuade them to give up sin. The primary objective for which the believer lives is to join in the battle against sin, and to seek the will and the honor of God. Let us be one with Christ and his Spirit in their testimony against sin. An exhibition of the life and Spirit of Christ in us will release holiness, love, joy, peace, and obedience to the Lord Jesus Christ, and convict the world of its sin and unbelief. The presence of Christ *in us* through the Spirit will carry its own conviction. And just as Christ's death was his sacrifice for sin, and was the entrance to his glory in the power of the Spirit, so too our experience of the Spirit's indwelling will become more complete as our entire life is given over to him for his holy work of convicting the world of sin.

PRAYER:

"Blessed Lord Jesus, it is by the presence and the power of the Holy Spirit in your people that the world is to be convicted of its sin of rejecting you, and that sinners are to be brought out of the world to accept you. It's in men and women full of the Holy Spirit, testifying in the power of a holy joy to what you have done for them, that the proof is to be given that you are indeed at the right hand of God. It's in a body of living witnesses to what you have done for them, that the world is to find the irresistible conviction of its sin and guilt.

"Lord, how little the world has seen of this. We call upon you, in deep humility, to make known to your Church the knowledge of its calling. Oh, that every believer in his personal

life and fellowship, might prove to the world what reality, what blessedness, what power there is in your faith! May the world believe that the Father has sent you, and has loved them as He loves you.

"Lord Jesus, please lay the burden of the sin of the world so heavy on the heart of your people that it may become impossible for them to live for anything but this - to be members of your body, in whom your Spirit dwells, and to prove your presence to the world. Take away everything that hinders you from manifesting your presence and saving power in us. Lord Jesus, your Spirit has come to us to convict the world - may he come and work in us in ever increasing power. Amen."

CHAPTER 13

WAITING FOR THE SPIRIT

He commanded them not to depart from Jerusalem, but to wait for the Promise of the Father, "which," He said, "you have heard from Me." Acts 1:4

I n the life of the saints of old, *waiting* was a common word which they used to express the attitude of their souls toward God. They waited *for* God, and waited *upon* God. Sometimes we see it in the scriptures as the language of an experience - *Truly my soul waits upon God, I wait for the Lord, my soul does wait.* At other times it is a plea in prayer - *Lead me; on You do I wait all the day. Be gracious unto us, we have waited for You.* Frequently it is an admonition, or an encouragement to perseverance in a time of difficulty - *Wait on the Lord; wait, I say, on the Lord. Rest in the Lord, and wait patiently for Him,* And then there is the testimony to the blessing of the exercise itself - *Blessed are they that wait upon Him. They that wait upon the Lord shall renew their strength.*

The Lord now uses this word, with all of its richness of meaning, in connection with the promise of the Father and the Holy Spirit. What has been so deeply woven into the life and language of God's people of old was now to receive a new and a higher application. Just as they waited for him to manifest himself, or intervene, or fulfill a promise in their lives, we also must wait for him. But now the waiting is for the fulfillment of the great promise in which the love of the Father and the grace of the Son are revealed and made ours through the indwelling gift of the fullness of the Holy Spirit. We wait on the Father and the Son for the ever increasing inflowing and working of the Spirit. We wait for the Spirit to move, and lead, and strengthen us. We wait for him to reveal the Father and the Son in us, and to work in us the holiness and the acts of service which the Father and the Son have called us to.

He charged them to *"wait for the promise of the Father, which you have heard from Me."* Do these words apply exclusively to the day of Pentecost, since the Spirit was given on that day, or are the words still valid for today; are we still waiting, and if so, what are we waiting for?

The questions and objections open the way to a very important lesson: ***The Holy Spirit is not given to us as a possession in which we have full control and can use at our own discretion, but he is given to us to rule over us, and to have control of us.*** We are not to use him, he is to use us. He is ours, but only ours as God's. This position is one of complete and total dependence on him who gives to every one *even as He will.* The Father has indeed given us the Spirit, but he works only as the Spirit of the Father. When we ask the Father to strengthen us with might by his Spirit, we must wait as surely and faithfully as if we were asking for the first time. When God gives us his Spirit, he gives his deepest inner self in the continuous, uninterrupted, and never ceasing power of eternal life. When Jesus promised rivers of living water to flow out of those who believe, he didn't speak of a single *act of faith* that would make them independent reservoirs, but of a *life of faith* that would always be receiving in, and giving out through a living union with him.

And so, *He commanded them to wait.* All of its meanings from the experiences of the past are now woven into the very fabric of the Holy Spirit's new indwelling life. What the disciples did and experienced during those ten days of waiting, and the fruit of what they received, becomes the pathway and the confirmation in which we are to live. The Father's promise of the outpouring, and the fullness of the Holy Spirit, and our waiting, are inseparably and forever linked together.

Could this be the reason why so many believers know so little of the joy and the power of the Spirit? They did not know to wait for it; they never listened to, or observed the Lord's parting words, *He commanded them to wait for the Promise of the Father, "which," He said, "you have heard from Me."* (Acts 1:4). They had heard of the promise, and they had pleaded for it in prayer to be fulfilled. They had been burdened and mourned under the weight of it; they believed for it and tried to lay hold of it, so that they could be filled with the Spirit. But they had never known what it was to wait. They had never said or truly heard, *Blessed are all they that wait for Him. They that wait on the Lord shall renew their strength.*

But what does it mean to wait? And how are we to wait? As a believer you are to wait for the full manifestation of the power of the Spirit within you. On the day of his resurrection Jesus breathed on his disciples and said, *"Receive the Holy Spirit,"* (John 20:22), and yet they still had to wait for the full baptism of fire and power.

As God's child you have the Holy Spirit in you. Please study the passages in Paul's letters that were addressed to believers who were full of all sorts of failings and sin, (see 1 Corinthians 3: 1-3, 16; 6:19, 20; Galatians 3:2-4, 6), yet who had the Holy Spirit. As you read of them in the scriptures, *begin* to cultivate in faith the quiet assurance, *the Holy Spirit is dwelling within me.* If you are not faithful in the lesser, you cannot expect to receive the greater. Acknowledge in faith and thanksgiving that the Spirit is in you. Each time you enter your place of prayer to speak to God, first be still and *believe* that the Holy Spirit is *within* you as the Spirit of prayer who cries, *"ABBA! Father!"* Stand before God in faith and boldly confess to him that you *are* a Temple of the Holy Spirit, until you become fully conscious of it yourself.

Now you are ready for the next step, which is to ask God simply, and right now, to give you the fullness of his Holy Spirit. The Spirit is in God, and in you. Ask the Father that his Spirit may come forth from him in greater life and power, and that the indwelling Spirit may work that life and power in you. Ask this on the ground of his promise, and believe that he hears you, and that he does it. Don't look to your heart to see if you feel anything - everything there may be dark and cold. No, believe and rest only in what God is going to do, and is already doing, whether you *feel* it or not. *Now comes the waiting.* Wait on the Lord, and wait for the Holy Spirit. Quiet your soul and be still before God, and give the Holy Spirit time to give you the deep assurance that God is giving the Spirit to work powerfully in you. It is the Spirit himself who will confirm what he is doing in you.

We are a *Holy priesthood to offer up spiritual sacrifices.* The slaying of the sacrifice was an essential part of the service. Each sacrifice you bring must be the surrender and the slaying of the self-life and its power of death. As you do so and wait before God, he sees in it that you have nothing - neither wisdom to pray, or strength to work. Waiting is the expression of need and emptiness. Throughout the Christian life these go together: the sense of poverty and weakness, and the joy of fullness and strength. It is in waiting before God that the soul sinks down into its own nothingness, and is then lifted up into the divine assurance that God has accepted its sacrifices and will fulfill its desires.

As you wait upon God, you continue in all the tasks and duties of your daily life, but in faith that God will fulfill his promises and meet your expectation. Give yourself to prayer and the reading of God's word, and ask the Holy Spirit to guide your prayers and thoughts. If you do not seem to be experiencing anything, don't become discouraged, but continue to wait with your simple surrender and faith. You have become so accustomed to worshipping in the power of your human understanding and your natural mind, that true spiritual worship does not come immediately. Keep waiting! *He commanded them to wait.* Maintain your waiting attitude in all of your daily life and work activities. *On You do I wait all the day.*

It is to the three-in-one God we speak - it is the Holy Spirit who brings him close and unites us to him. Renew and extend your faith each day, and continue your exercise of waiting upon God. The multitude of words and the fervency of feelings have often been a greater hindrance than help. God's work in you must become deeper, more spiritual, and more directly formed from God himself. Wait for the promise in all its fullness. Do not count the time that you wait as lost time. Anticipate that these expressions of humility, surrender, emptiness and faith will lead to your real and full surrender to the Lordship of the Spirit in your life.

Pentecost is meant to be the proof for all times of what the exalted Jesus does for his Church from his throne in heaven. The ten days of waiting is meant to be the posture that we take before his throne, which secures the Pentecostal blessing to flow continuously. The promise of the Father is sure, it is from Jesus that you have it. The Spirit is already working in you, his full indwelling and guidance is your inheritance as his child. Keep the words of the Lord! Wait on God, wait for the Spirit. *Wait, I say, on the Lord! Blessed are all they that wait for Him.*'

PRAYER:

"Blessed Father, from your beloved Son we have heard your promise. In a streaming forth that is divine and never ceasing, the river of the water of life flows from under the throne of God and the Lamb. Your Spirit flows down to bring life to our thirsty souls, For we have not heard, nor has our eye seen, what God has prepared for us that wait for Him.

"We have heard His charge to wait for the promise. We thank you for what has already been fulfilled to us of it. But our souls long for the full possession, the fullness of the blessing of Christ. Father, teach us to wait on you, to daily watch at the door post of your temple.

"Teach us each day, as we draw near to you, to wait for the Holy Spirit. In the sacrifice of our own wisdom and will, in holy fear of the workings of our own sinful nature, may we learn to lie in the dust before you, that your Spirit may work with power within us. Teach us, Father, that as our self-life is laid low before you each day, that the holy life that flows from beneath the throne will rise up in power and our worship will be in Spirit and in Truth. Amen."

CHAPTER **14**

THE SPIRIT OF POWER

"You shall be baptized with the Holy Spirit not many days from now... You shall receive power when the Holy Spirit has come upon you, and you shall be My witnesses..." Acts 1:5, 8

"But stay in the city... until you have been clothed with power from on high." Luke 24:49

The disciples heard John about the baptism of the Holy Spirit. Jesus spoke to them of the Father giving the Holy Spirit to those who asked him, and of the Spirit of their Father speaking in them. And on the last night he spoke of the Spirit dwelling in them, witnessing with them, and coming to them to convict the world of sin. They knew that the Holy Spirit would be central to the work they would have to do, and the power they would need for it. When the Lord Jesus summed up all his teaching in the promise, *"You shall receive power when the Holy Spirit has come upon you, and you shall be My witnesses,"* it must have been to them the summing up of what they were to look for - a new divine power for the new divine work of being the witnesses of the crucified and risen Jesus.

This confirmed all that they had seen in the scriptures of the Spirit's work. God had been striving with men from the days before the flood. He equipped Moses, and the seventy who received of his Spirit, for the work of ruling and guiding Israel. Later he gave wisdom to those who would build God's house, the Temple. In the days of the judges he gave them power to fight and conquer their enemies. In the times of the kings and the prophets, he gave them boldness to testify against sin, and power to proclaim a coming redemption. Every mention of the Spirit in the old testament is connected with the honor and the kingdom of God, and the equipping for service in it. In the great prophecy of the Messiah, which Jesus began his ministry in Nazareth with, (see Isaiah 61:1-2; Luke 4:18), his being anointed with the Spirit had the one purpose of bringing deliverance to the captives and gladness to those who mourn. To the minds of the disciples, as students of the old testament and followers of Christ, the promise of the Spirit could have only one meaning - being equipped and fitted for the great work they had to do for the Lord after he ascended to the throne. All that the Spirit would be to them personally in his work of comforting, teaching, sanctifying the soul, and glorifying the Lord Jesus, was only the means to their receiving power for the service of the call.

I pray that the Church of the Lord Jesus Christ understands this today! All prayer for the Holy Spirit's influence and guidance for God's children, should be so that we have the power to witness for Christ, and to conquer the world as he leads us. The waste of power is always a cause of regret to those who see it. The economy of power is one of the great moving principles in all organization and industry. The Holy Spirit is the great power of God and his redemption. Would he waste his power on those who only desire it for their own benefit, so that they can be good, holy, wise, or well known? No, the Holy Spirit is the power from God for carrying on the work for which Jesus sacrificed his own life. The essential condition for receiving this power is that we are found to be ready and fit for the work that the Spirit has come to accomplish through us.

"*My witnesses...*" These two words contain a divine and inexhaustible wealth of meaning. They are the perfect description of the Spirit's work, and our work - the work for which nothing less than his divine power is needed, and for which our weakness is now made strong. There is nothing quite so effective as an honest witness. Even the learned eloquence of the trial lawyer must give way to it. There is nothing quite so simple, just the telling of what we have seen and heard, or give witness and testify to what has been done in us. It was the great work of Jesus himself: "*For this cause I was born, and for this cause I have come into the world, that I should bear witness to the truth.*" (John 18:37). This is the same purpose of the power of the Holy Spirit in us, that we would be made witnesses of the truth in Jesus Christ. If we are to be his witnesses in the power of eternal life and the age to come, as he reigns in heaven, then we need his full power from heaven to strengthen the testimony of our lips and life.

The Holy Spirit makes us witnesses because *he* is a witness. "*He shall witness of Me,*" Jesus said. On the day of Pentecost, when Peter preached that Jesus Christ had ascended into heaven, had received the Holy Spirit from his Father, and had poured him forth, he spoke of what he knew - the Holy Spirit *witnessed* to him and in him, the glory of Christ. It was the same witness of the Spirit to the reality of Christ's power and presence that gave Peter great boldness and strength to speak before the council. "*God has exalted Him... to be Prince and Savior... and we are His witnesses to these things, and so is the Holy Spirit...*" (see Acts 5:31-32). As the Holy Spirit becomes to us divine life and power - the witness to what Jesus is at the present moment in his glory - *our* witness will be in his power. We may know everything that the gospels and the scriptures teach us of the person and the work of Jesus, but this is not the witness of the power that is promised here, and which will impact the world. It is only the presence of the Spirit in the present moment, witnessing to the presence of the personal Jesus, that gives our witness that breath of life from heaven, that makes it powerful for the casting down of strongholds. You can only be a witness *of* Jesus to the extent that the Holy Spirit is witnessing *to* you in life and truth.

The baptism of power, or the enduement of power, is sometimes spoken of, or sought after, as a special gift. Even though the Ephesians had been sealed with the Holy Spirit, Paul still prayed for them specifically that the Father would give them *the Spirit of Wisdom,* (see Ephesians 1:17). We cannot be wrong in praying distinctly for *the Spirit of Power.* He who searches our hearts knows what is the mind of the Spirit, and will give to us, not according to the correctness of our words, but according to the desires that the Spirit breathes into our hearts. In Paul's other prayer, (see Ephesians 3:14-17), he pleaded that the Father *...would grant us to be mightily strengthened by His Spirit.* In what ever way that we form our prayers, we know this much - it is on our knees and in prayer that we wait on God; he alone will bring what we ask, whether it is the Spirit of Power, or the power of the Spirit. The Spirit is not separate from God - in all things he is still the innermost self of God. It is God himself who, according to the riches of his glory, is powerful to do above and beyond all that we might ask or think, who will clothe us with the power of the Spirit in Christ Jesus.

As we seek the power of the Spirit, we need to understand how he works. The one mistake most believers make is that they expect to always *feel* the power when it works through them. On the other hand, scripture links power and weakness in a unique way, not as succeeding each other, but rather as existing together. *I was with you in weakness... my preaching was in power. When I am weak, then I am strong.'* (See 1 Corinthians 2:2-4; 4:7,16; 7:10; 13:3-4). The power is the power of God, given to faith, and faith grows in the dark. The Holy Spirit hides himself in the weak things that God has chosen, so that the flesh may not glory in his presence. Spiritual power can only be known by the Spirit of faith. If we confess our weakness and believe that the power dwells within us, and is available when needed, then we can expect to see it work more confidently, even when we *feel* nothing. Believers fail by not waiting for the power, and also by waiting incorrectly. We must combine faith and obedience to every act of service, with a deep, dependent, and expectant waiting for power, even if you *feel* nothing. Let your times of rest and communion be the exercise of prayer and faith in the power of God dwelling in you, and waiting to work through you. Your expectation in faith will bring the proof that out of weakness we are made strong.

Let us also understand the *condition* for the working of this divine power. It does not require much grace to long for, and ask for the power of the Holy Spirit. Who wouldn't be glad to have power? Many pray earnestly for the power of God for their work, but don't receive it, because they will not accept the only condition in which the power is able to work. *We* want to get possession of the power and use it - *God* wants the power to get possession of *us* and *use us!* If we give ourselves up to his power to rule *in us,* the power will give itself to us to rule *through* us. Unconditional submission and obedience to the power of God in our inner life is the *one condition* necessary to be clothed with it. God gives the Spirit to the obedient. Power belongs to God, and remains his forever. If you desire to have his power work in you, get low before his holy presence, which dwells in you. Surrender to his guidance, even in the least of things that come before you each day. Walk in humility and godly fear so that you will not fail to know him, or to do his will. If you live as one given up to a power that has complete possession of you, you will certainly know that his power works in you.

Let's also be clear as to the object of this power and the work it is to do. Men are very careful to economize power and to gather it where it can do its work most efficiently. God does not give his power for our own enjoyment, or to keep us from trouble and effort. He gives it for one purpose - to glorify the Son. Those who remain faithful in their weakness, and obedient to this one objective, who are ready at any cost to glorify God, are the ones who will receive power from God. God seeks men and women such as this whom he can fully cloth with his power. The Church is searching for them as well, marveling at the weakness and futility of so much of its ministry, movements, and worship. The world waits for it, waiting to be convinced that God is indeed in the midst of his people. The perishing billions are crying for deliverance from the powers of darkness, and God is waiting to work. Let's not just be content with the prayer for God to visit them and bless them, or with the effort to do the best we can for them. Let us give ourselves up completely, to live as witnesses for Jesus. Pray that God would show his people what it means to be Christ's representatives, just as he was the Father's. Let us live in faith that the Spirit of Power is within us, and that as we wait on him, the Father will fill us with the power of the Spirit.

PRAYER:

"Father, we thank you for the wonderful provision that you have made for your children, that out of our weakness we should be made strong, and that in our feebleness your mighty power should be glorified. We thank you for the Holy Spirit of Power, coming down to make Jesus, to whom all power is given, present with His Church and to make His disciples be the witnesses of that presence.

"I ask you, Father, to teach me that as I have the living Jesus, I have this power. May I not look for it to come with observation. And may I consent that it shall be a divine strength in my human weakness, so that the glory may be yours alone. May I learn to receive it in a faith that allows the mighty Lord Jesus to hold the power and do the work for me within my weakness. And may He be so present with me that my witness may be of Him alone.

"Father, I desire to submit my whole being to your holy power. I bow before its rule every day. I am willing to be its servant, and to humble myself to its most difficult commands. Father, let the power rule in me, that I may be made ready for it to use me. And may my one objective in life be that your Son would receive all the honor and the glory. Amen."

CHAPTER 15

THE OUTPOURING
OF THE SPIRIT

When the day of Pentecost had fully come... they were all filled with the Holy Spirit and began to speak... as the Spirit gave them utterance. Acts 2:1, 4

The work of Jesus Christ reached its climax at the outpouring of the Holy Spirit. His birth, his redemption for us on the cross, the revelation that he was the Son of God through his resurrection, and his ascension into glory, were only the preliminary stages of his work. Their crowning glory and his eternal goal was the coming down from heaven of the Holy Spirit. Pentecost is the last and the greatest of all the Christian feasts. In it all the other feasts find their realization and fulfillment. Because the Church has not fully understood or acknowledged this - that the glory of Pentecost is the greatest glory of God - the Holy Spirit has yet to fully reveal and glorify the Son in her as he would. Let's see if we can understand exactly what Pentecost means.

God made man in his own image and likeness, *that he should become like God.* (See Genesis 1:26). Man was created to be a temple for God to dwell in, and to become the home in which God himself would come and rest. This was to be the closest and most intimate union of all, the indwelling of Love in love. God longed for this, and looked forward to it. What was inadequately set forth in the example of the Temple in Israel, became a divine reality in Jesus of Nazareth. God had a man in whom he could rest, whose whole being was opened and submitted to the rule of his will, and the fellowship of his love. In Christ there was a human nature, possessed by the Spirit of God, who represented what God desired for all men to become. This became fulfilled in all those who believed in Jesus and his Spirit as their life. His death was to remove the curse and the power of sin, and to make it possible for them to receive his Spirit. His resurrection was the entrance of human nature - now free from all the weakness of the flesh - into the life of the deity, the nature of perfect fellowship with God in glory in the unity of the Spirit. And yet, even with all this, the work was not complete. There was more. Something was still waiting. How could the Father dwell in men even as he had dwelt in Christ? This was the great question to which Pentecost provides the answer.

Out of the fullness of God, the Holy Spirit was sent forth in a new nature and power. In creation and in nature he came as the Spirit of Life. In the creation of man especially, he was the power in which his divine character was grounded, and even after the fall, still testified for God. In Israel he appeared as the Spirit of the theocracy, distinctly inspiring and equipping certain men for their work. In Jesus he came as the Spirit of the Father, given without measure, dwelling, and remaining in him. All of these are manifestations, in different degrees, of one and the same Spirit. But now comes the long promised, the last, and an entirely new manifestation of the divine Spirit. The Spirit that dwelt in Jesus Christ and his life of obedience, has now taken up Christ's human spirit into perfect fellowship and union with himself, and is now the Spirit of the exalted God-man, Jesus Christ. As the man Jesus entered the glory of God, and the full fellowship of the Spirit in which God dwells, he received from the Father the right to send forth this same Spirit into his disciples. He would descend and dwell in them himself. In a new power, which had not previously been possible - because he had not been crucified or glorified - Jesus Christ descended as himself in the Holy Spirit, as the Spirit of the glorified Christ. The work of the Son and the longing of the Father was fulfilled.

Again, Pentecost is the greatest of all the feasts of God. The mystery of Bethlehem was incomprehensible and glorious, but once I believed it, there was nothing that appeared impossible. That a pure and holy body was formed for the Son of God by the power of the Holy Spirit, and that in that body the Spirit would come and dwell, is indeed a miracle. However, for the same Spirit to now come and dwell in the bodies of *sinful* men, and that the Father would come and make his home in them as well, is a mystery of such magnitude that it is beyond all understanding. But this is the very blessing that Pentecost brings and secures. As I said before, the entrance of the Son of God into our flesh in Bethlehem, his entering into the curse and death of sin as our substitute, his emergence in human nature as the first-born from the dead into the power of eternal life, and his entering into the very glory of the Father, were but the preparatory steps. The consummation for all of this was now the promise fulfilled: *Behold! The tabernacle of God is with men, and He shall dwell with them.* (Revelation 21:4).

It is only in the light of the great sacrifice which preceded Pentecost - in which God did not consider it too great for him to dwell with sinful men - that the narrative of the outpouring of the Holy Spirit can be understood. It is the earthly reflection of Christ's exaltation in heaven, and the participation he now gives to his friends of the glory he now has with the Father. To be fully understood it needs a spiritual revelation. In the story that is so simply told, the deepest mysteries of the kingdom are unfolded, and the title deeds are given to the Church of her holy heritage until Christ's return. What the Spirit is to be to believers and the Church, to the ministers of the word and their work, and to the unbelieving world, are the three main thoughts of this chapter.

1.) Every member of Christ own body is to be filled with Christ himself. Christ promised his disciples that in the Helper, he would come to them again. During his life on earth, his personal presence, and the revelation of the Father, was God's great gift to men; it was what they wished for and needed. But now, they were to receive something even greater in power than before. Christ had entered the glory with this very purpose, that now *He might fill all things,* that he might specifically fill every member of his body with himself and his glorified life. When the Holy Spirit came down, he brought the life of Jesus to live *within* them, which had previously only been a life *near* them, apart from their own. The very Spirit of God's own Son was now to become their own personal *life.* The same Spirit of Jesus who had lived, loved, obeyed and died, who had been raised from the dead, and was glorified by the power of God, was to now live in them. The glorious transaction that had taken place in heaven in the placing of their friend and Lord on the throne, was to be brought to them by the Holy Spirit, who would reveal it, witness of it, communicate it, and maintain it within them as a heavenly reality. It is no wonder that as the Holy Spirit came down from the Father, through the glorified Son, that their whole nature was filled to overflowing with all the joy and power of heaven. And with the presence of Jesus in them, their lives overflowed with the praise of the wonderful works of God.

This was the birth of the Church of Jesus Christ, and must be the source of its continued growth and strength. In order for the true Pentecostal Church (*see note at the end of this chapter) to thrive and grow in the earth, each true believer must be baptized with the Holy Spirit and fire. This is God's desire, and it is the only way for us to witness and testify by experience of the presence of Christ, who fills our hearts with the same glory and power that raised him from the dead and seated him in heaven with the Father. This is for every individual member of the body of Christ to know and possess, and witness of the presence of the indwelling Christ through the Holy Spirit. This is what will draw the attention of the world and compel the confession of the power of Jesus.

2.) Power and boldness has been given to his body to proclaim his life. It was in the middle of all the interest and the questions, which the sight of this joyous praising company of believers raised among the crowds, that Peter stood up to preach. The story of Pentecost teaches us the true position of the ministry and the secret of its power. A church full of the Holy Spirit is the power of God to awaken the careless, and attract all honest and earnest hearts. It is to an audience aroused by the testimony of believers, that the preaching will come with power. It is out of such a church of men and women, full of the Holy Spirit, that anointed preachers will rise up, bold and free, to point to every believer as a living witness to the truth of their preaching and the power of their Lord.

Peter's preaching is a remarkable lesson of what all Holy Spirit preaching should be. He preached Christ from the scriptures. In contrast with the thoughts of men, who had rejected Christ, he set forth the thoughts of God, who had sent Christ and who delighted in him, and had now exalted him at his own right hand. All preaching in the power of the Holy Spirit should be as Peter preached. The Spirit is the Spirit of Christ, the Spirit of his personal life, and takes possession of our personality, and witnesses with our spirit as to what all Christ has won for us. The Spirit has come for the purpose of continuing the work that the Lord Jesus Christ began on earth, which was to make men partakers of his redemption and life. It cannot be otherwise, the Spirit always witnesses of the Lord Jesus Christ - as he did in the scriptures, he now does in the believer - and the believer's true testimony will always be according to scripture. The Spirit in Christ, the Spirit in the bible, and the Spirit in the Church, is a threefold cord that is deeply intertwined and cannot be broken.

3.) The life and power of Christ in his people produces great results. The effect of Peter's preaching was powerful, but not more than should be expected. The presence and power of the Lord Jesus Christ was a present reality in the company of his disciples. The power from heaven had completely filled Peter, and the sight and experience that he had of Christ exalted at the right hand of God was such a spiritual reality that its power went out from him and reached the multitude. As he proclaimed, *"Know assuredly that God has made this Jesus, whom you crucified, both Lord and Christ,"* (Acts 2:36), thousands bowed in brokenness of spirit, ready to acknowledge the crucified one as their Lord. The Spirit had come to the disciples, and through them the multitudes were convinced of their unbelief. And as they heard the command to repent and believe, they also received the gift of the Holy Spirit. Jesus had done the greater works that he had promised to do through his disciples. In one moment in time lifelong prejudices, and even bitter hatred gave way to surrender, love and adoration. From the glorified Lord, power had filled his disciples, who were now his body, and from it power, has gone forth to conquer and save.

Pentecost is the glorious sunrise of *that day.* And the first of *those days* which the prophets and the Lord had spoken of so often. It is the promise and pledge of what the testimony of the Church is meant to be. It has been confessed by many that the Church has not fulfilled her true identity, that after so many centuries, she has still not risen to the height of her destined glory. Even when she strives to accept her calling to witness for her Lord to the ends of the earth, she does not do it in the faith of the Pentecostal Spirit, and the possession of his mighty power. No, instead of regarding Pentecost as a sunrise, she often speaks and acts as if it had been noon, from which the light began to fade. If the Church returns to Pentecost, Pentecost will return to her. The Spirit of God cannot take possession of believers beyond their capacity to receive him. The promise is waiting, the Spirit is now available in all his fullness. Our capacity to receive him needs to be enlarged. It is only in waiting in humility that Pentecost comes. We must continue to praise God in love and prayer, and in faith hold fast to the promise that he will make himself known to his people in power. His longing to reveal his presence in his disciples, and for them to participate in his glorified life, is as strong and fresh today as it was when he first ascended to the throne. Let us take our place in him, and yield ourselves in expectant faith, that we might be filled with the Holy Spirit and power, and testify of the Lord Jesus in us. Let the indwelling Christ be our life, our strength, and our testimony. Out of such a Church, believers who are filled with the Holy Spirit, will rise up with such power that the enemies of Christ will bow at his feet.

PRAYER:

"Lord God! We worship you before the throne on which you and the Son are seated, crowned with glory and honor. We thank you and bless you that it is for us, the children of men, that you have done this, and that He in whom you delight belongs as much to earth as to heaven, as much to us as to you!

"Father, we ask you to reveal to us how our head, the Lord Jesus Christ, counts us as his own body, and shares with us his life, and power, and glory; and how the Holy Spirit, as the bearer of that life and power and glory, is waiting to reveal it within us. Oh God, we pray that your people might awaken to know what the Holy Spirit truly means, as the real presence of the glorified Lord within them, and as the clothing with power from on high for their work on earth. We pray that we all might learn to look upon Jesus, the author and finisher of our faith, until our whole being is opened up to receive him, and his Spirit fills us to our full capacity!

"O Lord, we plead with you, in the name of Jesus, revive your Church! May every believer become a temple full of the Holy Spirit! May every church be a consecrated company, and its believing members ever testifying of a present Christ, and ever waiting for the fullness of power from heaven. We pray that everyone who preaches the word of God becomes a minister of the Spirit. And let Pentecost throughout the earth, be the sign that Jesus reigns, that his redeemed are his body, that his Spirit works, and that every knee shall bow to him. Amen."

*Note: Andrew Murray was not speaking in this chapter of what is known as the modern Pentecostal *movement*, but of the fullness that the Holy Spirit brings into man, the life of Jesus Christ in the glory and power of heaven.

CHAPTER 16

THE HOLY SPIRIT
AND MISSIONS

Now in the church that was at Antioch there were certain prophets and teachers... As they ministered to the Lord and fasted, the Holy Spirit said, "Now separate to Me Barnabas and Saul for the work to which I have called them." Then, having fasted and prayed, and laid hands on them, they sent them away. So, being sent out by the Holy Spirit, they went down to Seleucia, Acts 13:1-4

It has been said that the book of Acts might well have been named, The Acts of the Exalted Lord, or The Acts of the Holy Spirit. Christ's parting promise, *"You shall receive power when the Holy Spirit has come upon you; and you shall be My witnesses, both in Jerusalem and in all Judaea and Samaria, and unto the uttermost parts of the earth,"* (Acts 1:8), was a divine seed-word which contained the kingdom of heaven in the power of an infinite growth, with the law of its manifestation, and the prophecy of its perfection. In the book of Acts, we have the way traced out, and we see the promise fulfilled on its way from Jerusalem to Rome. It gives us the divine record of the coming and indwelling, and the working of the Holy Spirit as the power given to Christ's disciples. They were changed and transformed into witnesses for him before Jews and Gentiles alike, and they proclaimed the name of Jesus Christ from Antioch to Rome, as they were sent to the utter most parts of the earth. The book of Acts reveals that the primary aim and purpose of the descent of the Holy Spirit to his disciples was to equip them to be his witnesses even to the ends of the earth. He came as a light from heaven, revealing in them his presence, guidance, and power. Going forth to the lost souls of the world is the one object of the mission of the Spirit.

In Acts 13, we see the first record of the part that the Church is called to take in the work of missions. With Phillip at Samaria, and Peter at Caesarea, we have the record of individual men exercising their function of ministry, by the leading of the Holy Spirit, to those who were not Jews. In the preaching to the men of Cyprus and Cyrene, and to the Greeks at Antioch, we see the divine instinct of the Spirit of love and life, opening new paths previously unknown. The act of the Spirit separating special men was now to become part of the fabric and nature of the Church, with the entire community of believers educated and instructed to take its share of the work. If the second chapter of Acts is important in giving the Church power for her mission work in Jerusalem and Judaea, the thirteenth chapter is just as important for her being set apart for the work of missions. For our work in raising the Church to its true level of Pentecostal power to be permanent and personal, we must learn the lesson of Antioch. Missions work must find its direction and its power in the clear guidance of the Holy Spirit.

It has often been said that true mission work has always been born out of a time of revival in the Church. The Holy Spirit's quickening work stirs up a new devotion to the Lord Jesus Christ, and for those whom he longs to be his. It is in this environment that the voice of the Spirit is heard, urging his redeemed ones to go forth for him. This is what happened in Antioch. There were certain prophets and teachers there, who were spending time in fasting and ministering to the Lord. Along with their community service to the Lord, they spent time waiting on the Lord in separation from the world. They felt a great need for a closer and deeper fellowship with the him in their union with his crucifixion of the flesh. *They ministered to the Lord and fasted* was their posture before God, when the Holy Spirit said in the presence of the whole church, *"Separate unto Me Barnabas and Saul"* for that work.

The law of the kingdom of God has not been changed. It is still the Holy Spirit who is in charge of our mission work. And he still reveals his will, as regarding the who and the where of missions, to those who are separated and waiting on him.

In every generation the work and workers of missions are admired and honored as others see in them their love of God and how much they desire to serve him. It is easy to want to follow their example. And yet the genuine love, power, and devotion of these mission workers may be barely present. Because there is such great interest in missions, and yet so little direction and power evident in it, there is a great deal of exhorting, begging, and pleading on the ground level with its supporters. They usually only rely upon the command of the Lord as it is known and revealed in the written word; the living voice of the Spirit, who reveals the presence, power and direction of the Lord, has not been heard. It is not enough that believers are stirred and urged to take a greater interest in the work of missions, or to pray and give more - there is a more urgent need. In the life of the individual, the indwelling of the Holy Spirit, and the presence and rule of Christ must be the chief characteristic of their new life. In the fellowship of the Church, we must learn to earnestly wait for the Holy Spirit's guidance in the selection of men and women for missions, and their fields of labor, and in the wakening of interest, and in the seeking of support. If the missions and its workers originate through prayer and fasting, and wait on the Holy Spirit, we can expect that he will respond in direction and power.

Please don't think that we are trying to lead believers away from the real and practical work that needs to be done. There is much that must still be accomplished, and cannot be completed without people working. However, everything must be worked in the power of the Holy Spirit. This is the only way that it will be well pleasing unto the Lord. All our efforts outside of him account for nothing. Let me repeat that. All our efforts outside of him account for nothing! I pray that we might learn this vital lesson. The Spirit has come to us to be the Spirit of missions, to inspire and empower Christ's disciples to witness for him to the farthest regions of the earth. But the origins and success of missions are his alone. He is the one who stirs the hearts of believers with jealousy for his honor, with compassion for the lives of the perishing. As the man or woman *responds* in obedience to *his call*, and has faith in his promises, the mission stirs to life. It is the Spirit who opens the doors, and prepares the hearts of the unreached to desire and receive the word. And it is the Spirit, who in due time, gives the increase, plants the cross, and gathers around it those who are being saved. Even in the darkest strongholds of Satan's rule, if the mission and the called ones are from the Holy Spirit, then neither heaven or hell will be able to stop it.

Missions are the special work of the Spirit. No one can expect to be filled with the Spirit if they are not willing to be used for missions. And no one who responds to the work, or the prayer for missions, should ever fear in their weakness or poverty; the Holy Spirit is the power that prepares them to take his divinely appointed place in the work. Let everyone who prays for missions, and longs for more of a missionary spirit in the Church, first pray that in every believer personally, and the Church as a whole, in all of our work and worship, that we would be led by the fullness and the power of the indwelling Holy Spirit.

Then when they had fasted and prayed, they sent them away. And being sent forth by the Holy Spirit, they went down to Seleucia. The sending forth was equally the work of the Church and the Spirit. This is to be the normal relationship. There are those sent forth by the Holy Spirit alone, in the middle of great opposition or indifference, and the Spirit does his work. Then there are men and women sent forth by the Church, apart from the Holy Spirit;

work to be done has been identified, but there is little or no prayer and fasting, and it begins without the leading of the Spirit. The Church and the ones sent out are willing to work without the Spirit's leading and power. Blessed is the church that waits for him, and blessed is the mission which the Spirit originates, where he alone is allowed to guide.

After ten days of praying and waiting on earth, the Spirit's descent was in fire. This was the birth of the Church at Jerusalem. Ministering and fasting, and then again fasting and praying, the Spirit sent forth Barnabas and Saul - Antioch was the consecration of the Church to be a mission Church. Only in waiting and prayer on earth, and then in the power of the Spirit from heaven, comes the strength, and the joy, and the blessing of the Church of Christ for its missions.

May I say this to any current missionary who reads theses words in their mission field, *"Be of good cheer brother! Be of good cheer sister! The Holy Spirit, who is the mighty power of God, who is the presence of the Lord Jesus Christ within you, is with you, and he is in you! The work you are doing is his - depend upon him, yield to him, wait for him - the work is his, and he will accomplish it"*

And may I say to every Christian, whether you are working as a director, a supporter, contributor, prayer warrior, or in any other capacity for the kingdom of God, *"Be of good cheer!"* From the time of waiting before the throne, and the baptism received there, the first disciples went forth until they reached Antioch. There they paused, and prayed, and fasted, and then passed on over to Rome and the regions beyond. Let's learn from those early believers the secret of power. Let's call on every Christian who would be a missionary friend or missionary worker to come with us and be filled with the Holy Spirit, who is the Spirit of missions. Let's lift up a clear testimony that the true need of the Church and the world is believers who can testify to an indwelling Christ in the Spirit, and prove it as well. Let us gather together and wait as they did in the antechamber of the king's presence, as they did in the upper room in Jerusalem, and as they did in the ministering and fasting in Antioch. The Spirit still comes today in power as he did in those places, he still moves and sends forth. He is still mighty to convict of sin and to reveal Jesus, and to make thousands fall at his feet. He waits for us - let us wait for him, and let us welcome him.

PRAYER:

"O God! You sent your Son to be the savior of the world. You gave Him power over all flesh, that He should give eternal life to as many as you have given Him. And You poured out Your Spirit upon all flesh, commissioning as many as received Him to make known and pass on the wondrous blessing. He likewise sends forth those who yield themselves to Him, to be the instruments of His power in glorifying Your Son. We bless You for this divine and glorious salvation.

"Lord, we stand humbled by the neglect of Your Church in not fulfilling her divine commission. Forgive us for our slowness of heart to believe what Your Son promised, and to obey His will and finish His work. We cry to you, our God, visit Your Church and let Your Spirit, the Spirit of missions, fill all Your children!

"Father, I dedicate myself afresh to You, to live and labor, to pray and travail, to sacrifice and suffer for Your kingdom. I accept anew in faith the wonderful gift of the Holy Spirit, the very Spirit of Christ, and I yield myself to His indwelling. I humbly plead with You, for myself and all your children, that we would be mightily strengthened by the Holy Spirit, that Christ may possess our hearts and our lives, and that our one desire would be that they whole earth is filled with His glory. Amen."

CHAPTER 17

THE NEWNESS OF THE SPIRIT

Note: This chapter is a particularly difficult study of the Holy Spirit. Please pray before you attempt to grasp its meaning.

"Father, I pray that you would give me a spirit of wisdom and revelation that I might understand the spiritual truths contained here by the leading and anointing of the Holy Spirit, who lives in me. Protect me, Father, from trying to understand spiritual truths with my natural mind. I know that the natural man cannot understand spiritual things. Therefore, I ask you for spiritual wisdom that I might understand spiritual things in my spirit. Amen"

But now we have been delivered from the law, having died to what we were held by, so that we should serve in the newness of the Spirit and not in the oldness of the letter. Romans 7:6

But if you are led by the Spirit, you are not under the law. Galatians 5:18

The work of the indwelling Spirit is to glorify the Lord Jesus Christ, and to reveal him within us. Corresponding to Christ's three roles of prophet, priest and king, we find that the work of the indwelling Spirit in the believer has three purposes: *to enlighten, sanctify,* and **strengthen.** The Lord Jesus addressed the *enlightening* in his farewell message to his disciples, when he promised him, (the Holy Spirit), as the Spirit of truth, who bears witness of him, who guides us into all truth, and who takes what is of Christ and declares it to us. Then, in Paul's letters to the Romans and Galatians, his work as *sanctifier* is revealed - this was what was needed in new believers just brought out of the depths of sin and darkness. In his letters to the Corinthians, where wisdom was so sought after and prized, the two aspects were combined. They were taught that the Spirit can only *enlighten* as he *sanctifies*, (see 1 Corinthians chapters 2; 3:1-3; chapter 16:2; 2 Corinthians chapter 3). And in Acts, he was revealed as the *strength* they needed for the work before them. As the promised Spirit of power, he equipped them for a bold and anointed testimony in the middle of great persecution and difficulty.

Let's look at the letter that Paul wrote to the believers in Rome, who lived in the then known capital of the world. He gave them a full and systematic explanation of the gospel and God's plan of redemption, which the work of the Holy Spirit is central. In his words in the first chapter of Romans, *the righteous shall live by faith,* (Romans 1:17), he sets the foundation for what he was to expound, that through faith both righteousness and life would come. In the first part of his argument in verse 1, he teaches what the righteousness of faith is. He then proceeds to prove in verses 12-21, how this righteousness is rooted in our living connection with the second Adam, and in a justification of life. In the individual, (Romans 6:1-13), this life comes through the acceptance in faith of Christ's death to sin, and his life to God as ours, and our willing surrender to be servants of God and righteousness, (Romans 6:14-23). He then shows that in Christ we are not only dead to sin, but to the law as well, which is the strength of sin. He finally comes naturally to the new law, which the gospel brings to take the place of the old, the law of the Spirit of life in Christ Jesus.

An impression is often reinforced by the power of contrast. As Paul contrasted sin and righteousness in Romans 6:13, he then contrasts in Romans 7:4 the old and the new. The work and power of the Holy Spirit is to bring us out of the old, which keeps us in bondage to the letter of the law, and bring us into the new, in the liberty and power of Christ. In the following passages, (Romans 7:14-25; 8:1-16), we have the contrast worked out - it is in the light of that contrast alone that the two can be rightly understood. Each has its key-word, indicating the character of the life it describes. In Romans 7 the word *law* is used twenty times, and the word *spirit* only once. However, in Romans 8, the word *spirit* is used sixteen times. The contrast is between the Christian life in its two possible conditions - in the law, and in the spirit. Paul boldly states that we are not only dead to sin, and made free from it, that we might become servants of righteousness and to God, (see Romans 6), but also that *we were made dead to the law, so that, having died to that which we were held, we serve in newness of spirit and not in oldness of the letter.* We have here, then, a double promotion on the teaching of Romans 6. There it was the death to sin and freedom from it - here it is death to the law and freedom from it; there it was *newness of life,* (Romans 5:4), as an unbiased reality secured for us in Christ - here it is the *newness of spirit,* (Romans 7:6), as a personal experience made ours by the indwelling of the Spirit. He that would fully know and enjoy this life in the Spirit must also know what life in the law is, and how complete freedom from it has been made by the Spirit.

Paul describes the life of a believer still in bondage to the law, and trying to fulfill it, with several expressions that summarize its primary characteristics. The first is the word *flesh. "I am carnal,* (fleshly)*, sold under sin. In me, that is in my flesh, there dwells no good thing,"* (Romans 7:18). If we want to understand the word *carnal,* we must refer to Paul's commentary of it in 1 Corinthians 3:1-3. He uses it there to describe Christians who, though regenerated, (born of God), have not yielded themselves to the Spirit completely, and are carnal, or fleshly - they have the Spirit, but still allow their flesh, or carnal nature, to rule them. The difference between a carnal or spiritual Christian is who, or what, is the strongest in them - their flesh or the Spirit? If they have the Spirit, but have not fully accepted his powerful deliverance, and continue to strive in their own strength, *(flesh),* they are not, and cannot become spiritual - they are carnal. Paul says that the carnal ones *live* by the Spirit, but according to Galatians 5:25, do not *walk* by the Spirit. He has the new spirit within him, according to Ezekiel 36:26, but he has not asked for, or accepted God's own Spirit to dwell and rule within that spirit, as the life of his life. He is still carnal.

The second expression we find in Romans 7:18 is, *For I do not do what I want, but I do the very thing I hate,* (RSV). In every possible variety of expression in Romans 7, verses 15-21, Paul attempts to make clear the painful state of utter impotence, in which the Law, and the effort to fulfill it, leaves one a total failure - *For I do not do the good that I want to do, but I practice the evil that I will not want to do,* (verse 19). Willing, but unable to do, is the service to God in the old law of the letter, in the life before Pentecost, (see Matthew 26:41). The renewed spirit of man has accepted and consented to the will of God, but the secret of the power to do it, which is the indwelling Spirit, is not yet known. On the contrary, in those who know what the life in the Spirit is, God works both to will, and to do. The Christian testifies, *"I can do all things through Him who strengthens me,"* but this is only possible through faith and the Holy Spirit. As long as the believer has not consciously been set free from the law - with its *he that does all these things shall live through them* - failure will be the consistent result of his efforts to do the will of God. He may even delight in the law of God after the inward man, but the power to fulfill it is missing. It's only as he submits to the law of faith that he will know that he has been set free from the old law, and that he is joined to the living Jesus, who works in him through the Holy Spirit, so that he will bring forth fruit unto God. (See Romans 7:4).

Paul's final expression is in Romans 7:23, which says, *I see another law in my members (body) bringing me into captivity to the law of sin, which is in my members (body).* This word *captivity,* as the other one, *sold under sin,* suggests the idea of slaves sold into bondage, powerless to be free. They point back to what he had said in the beginning of the chapter, that we have been made free from the law, yet here is one who evidently does not know that liberty. And they point forward to what he says in Romans 8:2, *The law of the Spirit of life in Christ Jesus has set me free from the law of sin and death.* The freedom which we have in Christ, as offered through faith, cannot be fully accepted or experienced as long as there is any trace of a legal spirit. It is only by the Spirit of Christ within us that full liberation is realized. As in the old letter of the law, so in the newness of the Spirit, a twofold relation exists: the objective, (external), and the subjective, (personal). There is the law over me and outside me, the law of sin in my members, deriving its power from the first. Likewise, in being made free from the law, there is the objective liberty in Christ offered according to my faith. And there is the personal possession of that liberty, experienced in its fullness and power, to be had through the Spirit alone, dwelling and ruling in my members, even as the law of sin had done. This can change the cry of the captive from, *Oh, what a wretched man that I am! Who would deliver me from the bondage of this death?* (Romans 7:24), into the song of the redeemed, *I thank God through Christ Jesus our Lord. The law of the Spirit has made me free.* (Romans 7:25).

How should we regard the two states seen in Romans 7:14-23, and Romans 8:1-16? Are they interchangeable, successive, or simultaneous? Many have thought that they are a description of the varying experiences of the believer's life. As often as he is able to do what is good, by the grace of God, and to live well pleasing to God, he experiences the grace of Romans 8, yet the consciousness of sin, or his shortcomings, plunge him again into the failures of chapter 7. Though sometimes one or the other experience may be more prevalent, each day may bring the experience of both.

Others have felt that this is not the life of a believer according to the provision of God's grace. As they saw the life of freedom within their grasp through Christ, as the Holy Spirit dwelt within them, it was to them as if they had left the experience of Romans 7 far behind. They looked upon it as they would Israel's wilderness experience - a life left behind as they entered into the new. And there are many who can testify that they have, at times, experienced this new life.

And yet, however great the measure of truth was in their views, it does not fully satisfy. The believer feels that there is not a day that he or she gets beyond the words, *In me, that is, in my flesh, there dwells no good thing.* Even when joyfully living in the will of God, and strengthened, not only to will, but also to do, they know that it is not them, but the grace of God - for in me there dwells no good thing. And so the believer comes to see that there are not two experiences, but that the two conditions are simultaneous, and that even where his experience is mostly that of the law of the Spirit of life in Christ making him free, he still bears about with him the body of sin and death. The making free of the spirit, and the deliverance from the power of sin, and the song of thanksgiving to God is the continuous experience of the power of the endless life maintained by the Spirit of Christ. As I am led by the Spirit, I am not under the law. The spirit of bondage and its weakness through the flesh, and the sense of condemnation and the hopelessness it works, are cast out by the liberty of the Spirit.

If there is one lesson that the believer, who would enjoy the full indwelling of the Spirit, needs to learn, it is the one taught in this passage with such force - the law, the flesh, and all self-effort are utterly useless and incapable of enabling us to serve God. It is the Spirit within us that takes the place of the law outside of us, that leads us into the liberty in which Christ has made us free. *Where the Spirit of the Lord is, there is liberty.*

PRAYER:

"Beloved Lord Jesus, I humbly ask you to make clear to me the secret of the life of the Spirit. Teach me what it is, that we are to become dead to the law, so that our service to God is no longer in the oldness of the letter of the law. And teach us

that we are united to you, the risen One, through whom we bring forth fruit unto God, serving in the newness of the Spirit.

"Blessed Lord, with deep shame I confess the sin of my carnal nature, that 'in me, that is in my flesh, dwells no good thing, that I am sold under sin.' I bless you, that in answer to the cry, 'Who shall deliver me from this body of death?' you have taught me to answer, 'I thank God through Christ Jesus our Lord, the law of the Spirit of Life in Christ Jesus has set me free from the law of sin and death.

"Blessed Lord, teach me now to serve you in the newness and liberty of the Spirit of Life. Teach me to yield myself in full and wholehearted faith to the Holy Spirit that my life may indeed be in the glorious liberty of the children of God, in the power of an indwelling Savior working in me both to will and to do, even as the Father did work in him. Amen."

CHAPTER 18

THE LIBERTY OF THE SPIRIT

For the law of the Spirit of life in Christ Jesus has made me free from the law of sin and death… if by the Spirit you put to death the deeds of the body, you will live. Romans 8:2,13

The apostle Paul speaks in the sixth chapter of Romans, in verses 18 and 22, of our being set free from sin in Jesus Christ. Our death to sin in Christ has freed us from its dominion. When we accepted Christ in faith, we became servants, slaves if you will, to righteousness, and to God, free from sin as a power and our master. In the seventh chapter he speaks of our being made free from the law, (Romans 7:1-6). The strength, or power of sin is the law; deliverance from sin and the law go together. And having been set free from the law, we have been united to the living Christ, that in union with him, we might now serve in the newness of the Spirit. (See Romans 7:4-6). Paul presents our being set free from sin and the law as a life prepared in Christ, accepted and maintained by faith. According to the principle of a gradual growth in the Christian life, the believer must enter into this union, and then walk in it by faith, in the power of the Spirit with which he has been sealed. Most believers can testify that their life has not been what they had hoped it would be, even after they have seen and accepted this teaching; they have found the descent into the experience of the second half of Romans 7 to be very real and painful. It is because there is, generally, no other way to learn the two great lessons that the believer needs. The first is the great weakness of the human will, with the law urging it to obedience, to work out a divine righteousness through man's own efforts. The second is the need for the conscious and complete indwelling of the Holy Spirit as the *only* sufficient means and power for the new life of the child of God.

In Romans 8, Paul establishes this second truth. In the divine interpretation of the growth of the believers life in this letter, there are distinct steps to take. The eighth chapter introduces the Holy Spirit for the first time in the unfolding of the life of faith, and teaches us that it is only as the Holy Spirit influences our life and walk, are we able to fully possess and enjoy the riches of grace that are ours in Christ. Let every person who longs to know what it is to be dead to sin and alive to God, and to be united to Christ, come close to the Spirit of God. Let everyone who desires to be free from sin and the law, and experience union with Christ as a divine reality, embrace the work of the Holy Spirit. Then the life of Christ which is within us can be lived out in power and truth.

The key lies in Romans 8:2, *For the law of the Spirit of life in Christ Jesus has made me free from the law of sin and death.* It reveals the great secret of how freedom from sin and the law may become our reality. A believer may *know* that he is free from sin, and yet be forced to admit that his *experience* is still that of a slave. The freedom that he longs for is entirely *in* Jesus Christ, and the maintaining of our life-union with him is entirely the work of the Spirit's power. It is only as we see that the Holy Spirit dwells within us specifically for this purpose, and that we accept and yield to his working it out *in us,* that we can actually stand in complete freedom from sin. The life and liberty that Paul describes in Romans 6 and 7 are only fully ours as we can say, *"The law of the Spirit of life that is in Christ*

Jesus has set me free from the law of sin and death." Throughout the whole Christian life this principle rules: *"According to your faith be it unto you,"* (Matthew 9:29). As the Holy Spirit - who is the Spirit of faith - reveals the magnitude of God's resurrection power within us, and as our faith receives that power fully, all that is ours in Christ becomes true in our daily personal experiences. As the Holy Spirit reveals more and more of the revelation of our life in Christ, then the life of faith will open up to us, and free us from the law of sin and death. We learn that as perfect as is the life of liberty in Christ, so also is the power of that life in the Spirit, which enables us to walk in freedom. The assurance and experience of the Holy Spirit's indwelling will become our absolute necessity for this new life - he is inseparable from the person and the presence of the Lord Jesus Christ - he is the Spirit of Christ.

The law of the Spirit of Life in Christ Jesus has set us free from the law of sin and death. There are two opposing laws: one of sin and death in the members - our bodies - the other of the Spirit of Life ruling and raising up even the mortal body. Under the former, the believer is a hopeless prisoner of sin. But in the second half of Romans 6, Paul addressed him as being set free from sin, and by his voluntary surrender, becoming a servant to God and to righteousness. Yet, while he has forsaken his service to sin, it still often controls him. The promise that *sin shall not have dominion over you,* has not yet been realized. The will is present, but the knowing how to is not. *Oh wretched man that I am! Who will deliver me from this body of death?* is the cry of weakness and desperation in the midst of all failed attempts to keep the law. *I thank God, through Christ Jesus our Lord,* is the answer of faith that claims deliverance in Christ from this power of sin that has held him so captive. There is true deliverance from the law, (which is the dominion of sin and death), and its actual power in sin. That deliverance is a new law, a more powerful force which sets us free from sin. As real as the energy of sin is at work in us, even more powerful is the energy of the Holy Spirit, who dwells within us. It is the Spirit of Life that is in Christ which is now in us. Out of that resurrection life - which ascended to God, the eternal Spirit, and sits on the throne with him - descended the Holy Spirit, who is himself God. The law, and the power, and the dominion of the life in Christ has set me free from the law, and the power, and the dominion of sin and death in my mortal body, with a freedom that is as real as was my slavery. However, all of this was mostly caused by our ignorance for our need for his presence and great power. As the believer in Romans 7:14-23 was brought to the discovery of the deep-rooted legality of his old sin nature, and its absolute weakness, so the truth of the Holy Spirit and the power with which he sets us free from the power of sin and death is finally understood. Then our text becomes the declaration of the highest faith and experience combined: *The Law of the Spirit of Life has set me free from the law of sin and death.* As real, and powerful, and spontaneous was the law of sin in me, so now the Law of the Spirit of Life rules over me, and I am free!

The believer who would live fully in this liberty of the life in Christ, will easily understand and recognize the path which he must learn to walk upon. Romans 8 is the goal to which Romans 6 and 7 lead up to. In faith the believer needs to study and accept all that is taught in chapters 6 and 7 of his being in Christ Jesus, that he is dead to sin and alive to God, free from sin and a slave to God, free from the law, and united with Christ. *"If you abide in My word... you will know the truth, and the truth will set you free."* (See John 8:31, 32). Let the word of God, as it teaches you of your union with Christ, be the life-soil in which your faith and life dig their roots deep - abide in it, dwell in it, and let it abide in you. The way to rise and reach each higher truth that the scriptures teach is to meditate upon it, hold fast to it, and to patiently hide it in your heart in faith. And if the journey towards freedom from captivity appears at times to progress slowly, remember that it is only in the utter despair of our self-life that the complete surrender to the Spirit, who sets us free, is born and strengthened. The entry way into the liberty of the Spirit is only through our coming to an end of any hope in ourselves and our own efforts.

In order for us to walk on the path of this new life, we need to understand and remember what is meant by the expression

Paul used, *a walk after the Spirit.* The Spirit reveals the path to us, and leads us on it. This means absolute surrender and obedience - waiting to be led. He is to be our ruling power. We are to live and act under the law, the legislation, and the complete rule of the Holy Spirit in everything. Our lives must be marked by a holy fear of grieving him, a tender waiting on his leading, a deep faith in his hidden, but sure presence, and a deep adoration of him as God. Paul's words towards the close of this section should reflect our one aim: *If by the Spirit you put to death the deeds of the body, you will live.* (Romans 8:13). As the Holy Spirit possesses, inspires, and animates all the powers of our spirit and soul, entering even into the body, we are able to put to death the deeds of the flesh through the power of his divine life. This is our fulfillment of the word of God - *The law of the Spirit of the life in Christ Jesus has made me free from the law of sin and death.* This is the salvation and sanctification of the Holy Spirit, which we have been given.

We walk by faith is what we specifically need to remember in regard to a *walk after the Spirit.* The visible manifestation of the life of Christ and his work are so much more understandable than the revelation of the Spirit within us. It is here, as we seek the leading of the Spirit, that faith is called for. The Holy Spirit hides himself deep within us in the power of genuine union with our weakness. It requires faith and patience - to believe and obey - that we might come into the full consciousness of his indwelling life becoming our life. This understanding needs a flesh anointing every day from the Holy Spirit, in communion with Christ, and persevering in faith as we wait on the Father. Here the word is needed, *Only believe!* Believe in the Father and his promise! Believe in the Son and in his life as your own - *Your life is hidden in Christ in God!* (Colossians 3:3). Believe in the Holy Spirit as the bearer, communicator, and the keeper of the life and presence of Jesus! Believe in him as already within you! Believe in his power and faithfulness to work within you in a way that is divine and beyond your understanding. Believe that *the Law of the Spirit of Life in Christ Jesus has set you free from the law of sin and death.* Humble yourself in deep silence in your soul before God, and wait upon him to work deeply and powerfully in you by his Spirit. As we lay ourselves low before him, he will do his blessed and mighty work in us. He will reveal, and impart, and make, and keep, in his power, the Lord Jesus Christ as the life of your spirit.

PRAYER:

"My God and Father, I praise you for the wonderful gift of your Holy Spirit, through whom you and the Son have come to make your home in us. I bless you for the wonderful gift of eternal life, which your beloved Son brought to us, and which we have in the Lord Jesus himself, as his own life given to us. And I thank you that the Law of the Spirit of Life in Christ Jesus now sets us free from the law of sin and death.

"Father, I humbly pray and ask that you would reveal to us all in fullness, and in experience, what this perfect law of liberty is. Teach us how it is the law of an inner life, that in joyful and spontaneous power grows up into its destiny. Teach us that the Law of Christ is none other than that of eternal life, in its power of continuous and unfading existence. Teach us that it is the Law of the life of Christ Jesus, the living Savior himself, who lives and maintains it in us. Teach us that it is the Law of the Spirit of Life in Christ Jesus, the Holy Spirit, who reveals and glorifies Christ in us as an indwelling presence. Father, open our eyes and strengthen our faith, I pray, that we may believe that the Law of the Spirit of Life is indeed more powerful than the law of sin and death in us, and that we are free from it, that through the Spirit we have put to death the deeds of our bodies, and indeed live the Life of Christ.

"Father, teach all of this to me, and to all of your children! This I pray in Jesus name. Amen!"

CHAPTER 19

THE LEADING OF THE SPIRIT

For as many as are led by the Spirit of God, these are the sons of God. Romans 8:14

For many Christians, the leading of the Spirit is mostly looked upon as a suggestion of thoughts for our guidance. In the decision of questions of opinion or duty, or in the choice of words from scripture to use, or the distinct direction in performing some Christian work, most would welcome some leading from the Spirit. And at times when they think they have it, it still doesn't bring the assurance, comfort, or success that they think they should have if it was really from the Holy Spirit. And so the truth of the Spirit's leading, instead of being an end of all controversy, or the solution to all difficulty, or a source of comfort and strength, becomes instead a cause of perplexity, and the greatest difficulty of all.

This error comes from not accepting the truth that we have previously covered: the teaching and the leading of the Spirit is first given in the *life*, not in the conscious mind. The life is stirred and strengthened, then the life becomes light. As our conformity to this world and its spirit is crucified and dies, and as we deliberately deny the life of the nature of our flesh, we are renewed in the spirit of our mind, and the mind becomes able to test and approve the good, perfect, and acceptable will of God. (See Romans 12:1-2).

This connection between the practical sanctifying work of the Holy Spirit in our inner life, and his leading, comes out very clearly in the context of Romans 8:13, *If by the Spirit you put to death the deeds of the body, you shall live*; then immediately follows, *For as many as are led by the Spirit of God, these are the sons of God,* Romans 8:14. ***In other words, those who allow themselves to be led by him in the putting to death of the body, are the true sons of God.*** The Holy Spirit is the Spirit of the holy life, which is in Christ, and which works in us as a divine life and power. He is the *Spirit of Holiness,* and only in holiness will he lead us. Through him God works in us both to will and to do of his good pleasure. Through him God makes us perfect in every good work to do his will, working in us that which is well pleasing to him. To be led of the Spirit implies the complete surrender to his work as he convicts us of sin, and cleanses the soul and the body, and prepares them to become his Temple. It is his role as the indwelling Spirit - who fills, sanctifies, and rules the heart and the life - that he is able to enlighten and lead.

In studying what the leading of the Holy Spirit means, it is important to first grasp this thought in all of its significance. ***Only the spiritual mind can discern spiritual things, and receive the leading of the Spirit.*** The mind must grow spiritually in order to be capable of spiritual guidance. Paul said to the Corinthians, that even though they were born again, they were still carnal, babies in Christ, and that he was not able to teach them spiritual truth. If this is true of the teachings of men, how much more so of the direct teaching that comes from the Holy Spirit, by which he reveals all truth? The deepest mysteries of the bible, as far as they can be understood by human thought, can be studied and accepted, and even be taught by an unsanctified mind. However, as we have said before, the leading of the Spirit does not begin in our thoughts or feelings; the Holy Spirit abides and breathes deeper down, in the life itself, in the hidden recesses of our inner life. He brings the power that molds the will and fashions the character of our spirit, and then he moves, and compels, and leads. He leads by inspiring us with a disposition out of which right purposes come forth. *That you may be filled with the knowledge of His will in all wisdom and understanding,* Colossians 1:9. This prayer declares that it is only to a spiritual understanding that the knowledge of God's will can be given. Spiritual understanding only comes with the growth of the spiritual man, and with faithfulness to the spiritual life. He who would be led by the Spirit must yield himself to have his whole life fully possessed and filled with the Holy Spirit. It was only when the Lord Jesus Christ had been baptized with the Holy Spirit, *that being full of the Spirit, He was led by the Spirit into the wilderness,* (Luke 4:1), *that He returned in the power of the Spirit into Galilee,* (Luke 4:14), and began his ministry in Nazareth with the words, *The Spirit of the Lord is upon Me,* (Luke 4:18).

All leading implies that there is a following. It should be easy to understand that in order to experience the leading of the Holy Spirit, it demands a teachable and attentive spirit in us, and a willingness to follow him. The Spirit is not only hindered by the flesh, as the power that commits sin, but even more so by the flesh as the power that seeks to serve God. To be able to discern the Spirit's teaching, scripture tells us that the ear must be circumcised with a circumcision not made with hands, (the circumcision of the flesh), but in the circumcision of Christ. The will and the wisdom of the flesh must, above all things, be feared, denied, and crucified. Our ears must be closed to all that the flesh and its natural wisdom has to say, whether in ourselves, or in others. In all of our thoughts of God, or our study of his word, in drawing close to him in worship, or in our work for him, there must be a continued rejection of self, and a very definite waiting on God for the Holy Spirit to teach us and lead us. The soul that waits daily, even hourly, for divine leading, for the light of knowledge, or for its duty, will most certainly receive it. If you desire to be led by the Spirit daily, in every circumstance, then give up not only your will and wisdom, but your whole life and being. Then the fire will descend and consume the sacrifice.

The leading of the Spirit must be specifically a matter of faith. The beginning of the leading will come when we learn to cultivate and act upon this confidence - in the fear of the Lord, the Holy Spirit is in me, and is doing his work. The Spirit's indwelling is the crowning piece of God's redemption work. It is the most spiritual and mysterious part of the mystery of godliness. Faith is needed here more than anywhere else. Faith is the faculty of the soul which recognizes the unseen and the divine, and which receives the impressions of God's presence when he draws near. Faith, in its fullness, accepts what he brings and gives to us. The Holy Spirit carries and presents to us the most intimate communication of the divine life. Here, faith does not judge by what it feels or understands, but it simply submits to God to let him do what he has said. It meditates and worships, prays and trusts daily, and it yields the entire soul to richly accept, with great thanksgiving, the words of the Lord, *He shall be in you.* It rejoices in the assurance that the Holy Spirit, the power of God, fully dwells in us in his own way. He will lead me, and I can depend upon that.

Then, beyond a general faith that the Spirit indwells us, faith must also be exercised in regard to each part of his leading. When I ask the Lord a question, and empty my soul, and wait in humility for his revelation or will to be given me, I must trust that his leading and guidance will come. We cannot expect the Spirit's leading to come in sudden impulses, or strong impressions, in heavenly voices, or even in remarkable encounters. There are some who are led in this way, and the time may come as our nature becomes spiritual, and we live in more direct contact with the invisible, that our very thoughts and feelings bear the consciousness of his voice. But let us leave that and the growth of our spiritual capacity up to him. The steps of the ladder are low enough for even the weakest believer to reach. God desires for each of his children to be led by the Spirit every single day. Begin the path of following the Spirit's leading by believing, not only that he is within you, but that he is now beginning the work which you have asked him to do. Yield yourself to God in full surrender, and believe with complete confidence that his acceptance of your surrender means that you are now living under the charge and control of the Holy Spirit. Through him the Lord Jesus now guides, rules over you, and saves you.

But aren't we in danger of being led astray by the empty imaginations of our own hearts, when we think something is the leading of the Holy Spirit, but it's actually a delusion of our own minds? And if so, where is our safeguard from this error? The answer ordinarily given would be the word of God. And yet that is only half the truth. Far too many have used the bible to oppose the danger of fanaticism, but have done so by interpreting the scriptures through their own human understanding, therefore erring just as much as those they oppose. The truth is this - it is the word of God as taught by the Spirit of God. It is the perfect harmony of the two - the word and the Spirit - that our safety is to be found. Let us remember that as all the word of God is given by the Spirit of God, so each word must be interpreted to us by that same Spirit, This interpretation comes to us from the *indwelling* Spirit, not from the Spirit *above* us, or *around* us. It only comes from the Spirit *within* us, and only in the spiritual man or woman whose inner life is under the control of the Spirit. This is the one who can discern the spiritual meaning of the word of God.

On the other hand, let us hold fast that as all the word is given by the Spirit, so his great work is to honor that word, and unfold the fullness of the divine truth treasured there. Not in the Spirit without the word, and not in the word without the Spirit, but in the word and the Spirit, both indwelling within us richly, are we assured of the complete safety in the Spirit's leading and guidance, as we yield ourselves to him in full surrender and obedience.

This brings us back to the lesson we urged at the beginning of this chapter - the leading of the Spirit is inseparable from the sanctifying work of the Spirit. Let each one of us who would be led by the Spirit begin by giving ourselves over to be led by the word, as far as we know it. Begin at the beginning - obey his commandments. *"He that will do, shall know,"* said Jesus. *"Keep my commandments, and the Father will send you the Holy Spirit."* Give up every sin; give up everything to the voice of conscience; give up everything to God, and let him have his way in you. Through the Spirit put to death the deeds of your body, (Romans 8:13). As a son of God, place yourself at the complete disposal of the Spirit, and be willing to follow where he leads you, (see Romans 8:14). And this same Spirit through whom you put to death sin, and surrendered yourself to be led as a son, will witness, and confirm with your spirit, in a joy and power previously unknown, that you are indeed a son of God, who is led by the Spirit, and who is free to enjoy all of a child's privileges in his Father's love and guidance.

PRAYER:

"Father, I thank you for the message that as many as are led by the Spirit of God, these are the sons of God. You would not have your true sons led by anyone, or anything, other than your own Spirit. As he dwelt in your Son, and led him, so he leads us too with a divine and blessed leading.

"Father, you know how by reason of our not rightly knowing and not perfectly following the guidance of the Holy Spirit, we are often unable to know his voice, so that the thought of his leading is sometimes more of a burden than a joy. Forgive us, O God! Please quicken our faith in the simplicity and certainty of the leading of the Spirit, that with our whole heart we may yield ourselves, from here on in, to walk in it.

"Father, I hereby yield myself to you as your child, to be led by your Spirit in all things. I relinquish my own wisdom and will, and I desire to wait daily in complete dependence for your guidance through the Holy Spirit. May my spirit be silent before your holy presence, while I wait to let your indwelling Spirit rule me from within. As I continue to put to death, through the Spirit, the deeds of my body, may I be

transformed in the renewing of my mind, that I might know your good, perfect, and acceptable will. May my whole being be under the rule of the indwelling and sanctifying Spirit, that my spiritual understanding of your will may indeed be the rule of my life. Amen."

CHAPTER 20

THE SPIRIT OF PRAYER

Likewise the Spirit also helps in our weaknesses. For we do not know what we should pray for as we ought, but the Spirit Himself makes intercession for us with groanings which cannot be uttered. Now He who searches the hearts knows what the mind of the Spirit is, because He makes intercession for the saints according to the will of God. Romans 8:26-27

Of all the works of the Holy Spirit, the one that leads us the deepest into God's grace, and into the mystery of the Godhead, is his work as the Spirit of prayer. It is in Christ that we are in union with God, and through him we pray and receive the answers to our prayers. And we have the Holy Spirit in whom we pray, who prays in us according to the will of God. His prayers are with deep and hidden groans which can barely be uttered, so much so that God has to search our hearts to know what is in the mind of our spirit. As wonderful and as real is the divine work of God on the throne, hearing and powerfully answering prayer; and as divine as is the work of the Son interceding, securing, and transmitting the answers from above, so also is the work of the Holy Spirit in us, in the prayer which waits and obtains the answer. We need to understand that the intercession within is as divine as the intercession above.

In the creation it was the Spirit who hovered over the dark and lifeless matter of chaos, and by his life giving energy imparted the power of creation and fruitfulness. It was only after it had been given life by the Spirit, that the word of God gave it substance, and called forth all the different forms of life and beauty that we now see. Likewise, in the creation of man, it was the Spirit that was breathed into the body that God had formed from the ground, and united himself to what would have otherwise been lifeless matter. And in the person of Jesus, it was the Spirit who prepared a body for him, and it was through the Spirit that his body was brought back to life from the grave. It is through this same Spirit that our bodies are prepared and made ready to become the temples of God, and members of the body of Christ. We think of the Spirit only as in connection with the spiritual nature of the divine being, far removed from the weakness and grossness of matter. But we forget that the specific work of the Spirit is to unite himself with the creation, and to raise it up into his own spirit-life and nature, and develop in us the highest form of perfection - a spiritual body.

This view of the Spirit's work is essential in understanding the place he takes in the divine work of redemption. In each part of our redemption there is a special place assigned to each of the three persons of the Godhead. The Father is the unseen God, the author of all; in the Son of God, we have the form of God revealed and manifested, and brought close to us; and in the Spirit of God, we have God in us, the power of God dwelling in the human body, and working in it all that the Father and the Son have for us. Only through the intervention and operation of the Holy Spirit can what the Father purposed, and the Son obtained, be appropriated and take effect, not only in the individual, but in the Church as a whole.

This is especially true of intercessory prayer. The coming of the kingdom of God, the increase of grace, knowledge, and holiness in believers, and their growing devotion to God's work, and the working of God's power on the unconverted through the means of grace - all awaits us from God through Christ. However, it will not come unless it is looked for and desired, asked for and expected, and believed for and hoped. This is the key position that the Holy Spirit now occupies. His purpose is to prepare the body of Christ so that it is ready to receive all the fullness of Christ, who is our head. Both the Son and the Spirit work to communicate to us the Father's love and blessing. The Son receives from the Father and reveals it, and brings it close to us, then the Spirit from within us awakens the soul to meet its Lord. As indispensable as the unceasing intercession of Christ from above us is, asking and receiving from the Father, so too is the unceasing intercession of the Holy Spirit from within us, asking and accepting from the Son what the Father gives.

The words of Romans 8:26-27 sheds God's light upon this holy mystery. In the life of faith and prayer there are operations of the Spirit in which the word of God is made clear to our understanding, and we know how to express and ask for what is needed. But there are also operations of the Spirit which are deeper than thoughts or feelings, where he works in us desires and yearnings in our spirit, in the secret springs of our life and being, which only God can discover and understand. This is the place in our spirits where our real thirst is for God himself, and our longing to know his love, *which surpasses all understanding, that we might be filled with all the fullness of God, and the hope in him who is able to do exceedingly abundantly above all that we can ask or think, and even what has not entered into the heart of man to conceive.* (See Ephesians 3:19-20). When these longings and desires take possession of us, we begin to pray for what can hardly be expressed, and our only comfort is that *then* the Spirit prays with his unutterable and indiscernible yearnings, in a language which he alone knows and understands.

To the Corinthians Paul said, *I will pray with the Spirit, and I will pray with the understanding as well.* Under the influence of the moving of the Holy Spirit and his miraculous gifts, the danger was to neglect the understanding. Our danger in these latter days is the opposite - praying with our understanding is universal and easy.

We need to be reminded that with the prayer of understanding, there must also come prayer with the Spirit - *praying in the Holy Spirit,* (see Jude verse 20; Ephesians 6:18). A proper place must be given to each of the operations of the Spirit. God's word must dwell in us richly, and our faith must hold it clearly and intelligently, and to plead for it in prayer. To have the words of Christ abiding within us, filling our lives and influencing our conduct, is one of the secrets of acceptable prayer. However, we must also remember that in the inner sanctuary of our being, in that region of the unutterable and inconceivable, (see 1 Corinthians 2:6), the Spirit prays for us what we do not know or understand, and cannot express. As we grow in our understanding of the Holy Spirit, both his divinity, and the reality of his indwelling, we will begin to recognize the divine hunger with which he draws us heavenward. As our faith grows, and as we seek to grasp and obey God's word, we will learn to pray, understanding how infinitely above is God and the spirit world. When our heart and flesh fails us, God is our strength through the Holy Spirit dwelling within us in the innermost sanctuary of our spirit. There within the veil he does his unceasing work of intercession, and prays according to the will of God within us. As we pray, let us worship in holy stillness, and yield ourselves to the one who comes alongside us, our helper, the Spirit of intercession.

Because He makes intercession for the saints... Why doesn't Paul say for us, as he had said previously, *We know not how to pray as we ought?* The expression *the saints* is one of his favorites, when he refers to the Church. The special work of the Spirit, as he dwells in every member, is to make the body realize its unity. It is as selfishness disappears, and the believer becomes more truly spiritually minded, and identifies more with the body as a whole, regarding its health and well being as his own, that he learns what it means to *pray at all times in the Spirit, with all perseverance for all the saints.* As we give up ourselves wholeheartedly for this work, which encompasses the entire body of Jesus Christ, the Spirit will have the freedom to do his work of intercession for the saints in us. It is particularly in intercessory prayer that we may count upon the deep, unutterable, but all prevailing intercession of the Holy Spirit.

What a privilege we have to be the temple of the Holy Spirit, from which he cries to the Father his unceasing *Abba,* and offers his, too deep for words, unutterable intercession. As the eternal Son dwelt in the flesh in Jesus of Nazareth, and prayed to the Father as man, we are now blessed that the eternal Spirit dwells in us, sinful flesh, to train us to speak with the Father, even as the Son did. Who would not be willing to yield himself to this blessed Spirit, to be made fit to take part in the mighty work of intercession, through which alone the kingdom of God can be revealed? The path is open and the invitation is for everyone who believes. Let the Holy Spirit have full possession of you. Let him fill you completely. Let him be your life. Believe with your whole being in the possibility of his making your very personality and consciousness his dwelling place. Believe that he will work in you, and pray through you, beyond what your human mind can understand. And finally, believe that in the faithfulness of that work, his power is perfecting within you the divine purpose of your union with the Lord Jesus Christ. Live as one in whom the things that surpass all understanding have become truth and life, and in whom the intercession of the Spirit is part of your daily life in Christ.

PRAYER:

"Most Holy God, I am beyond words as I bow in love and adoration to you, in your presence. I thank you for the precious privilege of prayer. And I especially thank you for the grace that has not only given us in your Son as our Intercessor, but also your Spirit, who is the intercessor who lives within us.

"Father, you know that I can hardly take in the wonderful thought that your Holy Spirit indeed dwells in me, and prays through my weak and frail prayers. I beseech you, reveal to me anything that might hinder the Spirit's taking complete possession of me, and of his filling me with the consciousness of his presence. Let my inmost being and my outer life be fully

under his leading, that I might have the spiritual understanding to know your will in all things, and the living faith that receives what it asks.

"And Father, when I don't know what or how to pray, teach me to be silent and worship you, and wait for you, knowing that the Spirit breathes the wordless prayers which you alone understand.

"Oh God, I am a temple of the Holy Spirit, and I yield myself for him to pray out of me as the Spirit of intercession. May my whole heart be so filled with the longing for Christ's honor, and his love for those who don't know him, that my life may become one unutterable cry for the coming of your kingdom. Amen."

CHAPTER 21

THE HOLY SPIRIT AND CONSCIENCE

I am telling the truth in Christ, I am not lying, my conscience testifies with me in the Holy Spirit. Romans 9:1 (NASB)

The Spirit Himself testifies with our spirit. Romans 8:16 (NASB)

God's highest glory is his *holiness,* from which he hates and destroys evil, and loves and works good. In man, conscience has the same purpose. It condemns sin and approves what is right. Conscience is the remnant of God's image in man, the nearest approach to the divine in him, and the guardian of God's honor in the midst of the ruin of man's fall. As a consequence, God's work of redemption must always begin with the conscience. The Spirit of God is the Spirit of his holiness, and conscience is a spark of that divine holiness. Harmony between the work of the Holy Spirit in renewing and sanctifying man, and the work of conscience, is both intimate and essential. The believer who desires to be filled with the Holy Spirit and experience all of the fullness that he has to give, must first see to it that he yields to his conscience the place and the honor which belongs to it. Faithfulness to conscience is the first step in the path of restoration to the holiness of God. Intense conscientiousness will be the groundwork and the characteristic of true spirituality. It is the work of our conscience to testify to our being right towards God, and in our actions; it is the work of the Spirit to testify to God's acceptance of our faith in Christ and our obedience to him. As our life in Christ progresses, the testimony of the Spirit and our conscience will become increasingly identical. We shall know the joy of saying with Paul, *My conscience testifies with me in the Holy Spirit.*

Conscience can be compared to the window of a room, through which the light of heaven shines in, and through which we can look out and see heaven and all that its light shines upon. The heart is the chamber in which our ego - or soul life - dwells, with all of its powers and affections. On the walls of that chamber is written the law of God. Even in the unbeliever it is still partly legible, though darkened and disfigured. In the one who believes, the law is written once again by the Holy Spirit, in letters of light; they may be dim at first, but grow brighter and clearer as they are exposed to the power of the God's light. With every sin that I commit, the light that shines into me reveals it and condemns it. If the sin is not confessed and turned away from, its stain remains within me, and my conscience becomes soiled and defiled, because I refused the teaching of the light, (see Titus 1:15). And with each additional sin the window turns darker and darker until the light can barely shine through at all. As I continue in sin, I become so blinded and desensitized that my conscience no longer bothers me. In his work of renewal the Holy Spirit does not create new facilities, he renews and sanctifies those already existing. Conscience is from the Spirit of God, the Creator. As the Spirit of God, the Redeemer, he first redeems what sin has defiled. It is only in restoring conscience to its full and healthy place, revealing to it the wonderful grace of Christ - *the Spirit testifies with our spirit* - that he enables the believer to live a life in the fullness of God's light. As the window of the heart looks towards heaven and is cleansed, and remains clean, then we are able to walk and remain in God's light.

The work of the Holy Spirit on our conscience is threefold. Through conscience the Spirit causes the *light of God's holy law* to shine into the heart. A room may have its curtains drawn, and its blinds closed, but this cannot keep the flash of lightning from piercing into it from time to time. The conscience may be so sin-stained and seared that the *strong man* within resides there in perfect peace, but when God's lightning flashes into the heart, conscience wakes up, and is immediately ready to admit and sustain the conviction. Both the law and the gospel, with their call to repentance and their conviction of sin, appeal to the conscience. But it is not until the conscience has said *"Amen"* to the charge of sin and unbelief that true deliverance can come.

It is also through conscience that the Spirit causes the light of mercy to shine. When the windows of a house are dirty, they need to be washed. How much more shall the blood of Jesus wash and clean our conscience? The whole aim of the blood of Christ is to reach the conscience and silence its accusations, and thoroughly clean it until it testifies that *every stain has been removed and the love of the Father pours in through Christ in unclouded brightness into my soul. A heart sprinkled from an evil conscience, having no more conscience of sin,* (see Hebrews 9:14, and 10:2, 22), is meant to be the privilege of every believer. It becomes so when our conscience learns to say *"Amen"* to God's message of the cleansing power of the blood of Jesus.

The conscience that has been cleansed in the blood of Jesus must be kept clean by walking in faithful obedience in the light of God's favor. The conscience must say its *"Amen"* to the promise and willingness of the indwelling Spirit to lead us in all God's will. The believer is called to walk in humility and tenderness, watchful that even in the slightest of things, his conscience would convict him for not doing what he knows is right, or doing that which is not of faith. (See Romans 14:23). May we be content with nothing less than Paul's joyful testimony, *Our glorying is this, the testimony of our conscience, that in holiness and godly sincerely, by the grace of God, we behaved ourselves in the world,* (2 Corinthians 1:12). Let us note these words well, *Our glorying is this, the testimony of our conscience.* As the window of our conscience is kept clean, as the love of God's light shines in us, and as we walk in that love, then we will have fellowship with the Father and the Son. *Beloved, if our hearts do not condemn us, we have boldness toward God, because we keep His commandments, and do those things that are pleasing in His sight,* (1 John 3:21-22).

The maintenance of a good conscience towards God and man is essential to the life of faith. The believer must be satisfied with nothing less than it, and be assured that it is within his reach. In the old testament the saints had the testimony, through faith, that they pleased God. (See Hebrews 11:4-6, 39). In the new testament it is set before us as a commandment to be obeyed, but also as a grace to be worked by God himself. *That you may walk worthy of the Lord, fully pleasing Him, strengthened with all might according to His glorious power,* (Colossians 1:10-11) *May God fulfill all the good pleasure of His goodness, and the work of faith with power,* (2 Thessalonians 1:11). *Working in us that which is well pleasing in His sight,* (Hebrews 13:21).

The more we seek the testimony of conscience, that we are doing what is well pleasing to God, the more we shall feel the liberty, even in failure, to look immediately to the blood of Jesus that always cleanses us. We will become more confident that the sin that dwells within us, with all its unknown workings, is covered by his blood as well. The blood that has sprinkled the conscience abides and acts there in the power of the eternal life that takes no rest. *If we walk in the light as He is in the light, we have fellowship with one another, and the blood of Jesus cleanses us from all sin,* (1 John 1:7).

The cause of our weak faith is directly linked to our lack of a clear conscience. Look at how closely Paul connects them in 1 Timothy, *Love from a pure heart, and a good conscience, and from sincere faith, (1:5), having faith and a good conscience, which some have rejected, concerning the faith have suffered shipwreck, (1:19).* And especially 1 Timothy 3:9, *Holding the mystery of the faith with a pure conscience.* The conscience is the seat of faith. If we desire to grow strong in faith, and have boldness with God, we must be confident that we are pleasing to him, (see 1 John 3:21-22). Jesus said very clearly that it is for those who love him, and keep his commandments, that the promise of the Spirit, and the indwelling of the Father and the Son are meant for. (See John 14:23).

How can we confidently claim these promises unless our conscience can testify in that we have faithfully fulfilled his conditions? The body of Christ must rise up to its high and holy calling as intercessor, and claim these unlimited promises as being within its reach. Believers must continue to draw near to their Father, in the testimony of their conscience, that by the grace of God they are walking in holiness and godly sincerity. We must see that this is the deepest humility and brings the most glory to God's free grace - the giving up of man's ideas of what we can attain, and accept God's declarations of what he desires and has promised - as the only standard of what we are to be.

How are we to attain this life where we can daily appeal to God and men as Paul did - *I say the truth in Christ, my conscience bears me witness in the Holy Spirit?* Our first step is to get very low under the conviction of our conscience. We can't be content with a general confession that there is a great deal wrong. We can't confuse actual transgressions with the temptations of sin. If the temptations are to be conquered and made dead by the indwelling Spirit, (Romans 8:13), we must first deal with the sins themselves. Begin with some single sin, and give your conscience time in silent submission and humility to reprove it and condemn it. Say to your Father that in this one thing, by his grace, you are going to be obedient. Accept once more Christ's wonderful offer to take complete possession of your heart, and to dwell in there as Lord and keeper. Trust him by his Holy Spirit to do this, even if you feel weak and helpless. If you allow the words of Christ to dwell in you richly, and obey them, you will demonstrate to him your full surrender and your interest in his will and grace. Declare in faith that by God's grace you will always seek to have a conscience free of offense towards God and man.

When you have taken this first step with one sin, then continue step by step with others. As you are faithful to keep your conscience pure, God's light will shine more brightly into your heart, revealing sin that you had not noticed before. Be willing to be taught, and be confident that the Spirit will teach you. As you yield yourself completely to his power and will, the Holy Spirit will help you with your faithful effort to keep your conscience clean.

As you submit to the reproofs of your conscience and give yourself fully to do God's will, you will begin to believe that it is truly possible to have a conscience free of offense. The witness of your conscience, as to what you are doing and will do by grace, will be met by the witness of the Holy Spirit, as to what Christ is doing and will do. Begin each day with these words of prayer: *"Father, there is now nothing between you and me. My conscience, which has been cleansed by the blood of Christ, bears witness to me. Father, do not let even the shadow of a cloud intervene with us today! In everything I desire to do your will; your Spirit dwells in me and leads me, and makes me strong in Christ."* Do this and you will enter into the life which glories only in God's grace when it says at the end of each day, *Our glorying is this, the testimony of our conscience, that in holiness and godly sincerely, by the grace of God, we have behaved ourselves in the world. My conscience bears me witness in the Holy Spirit.*

PRAYER:

"Gracious Father, I thank you for the voice of conscience that you have given us in our hearts, to testify whether we are pleasing to you or not. I thank you that when the witness within convicts me with its terrible 'Amen' to the curse of your law, that you gave the blood of your dear Son to cleanse my conscience. I thank you that at this moment my conscience can say 'Amen' to the voice of the blood, and that I may look unto you in full assurance, with a heart cleansed from an evil conscience.

"I thank you also for the Holy Spirit, the witness from heaven to what Jesus has done, and is doing for me, and in me. I thank you that he glorifies Christ in me, and gives me his presence and power, and transforms me into the image and likeness of the Lord Jesus Christ. I thank you that in the presence and the work of your Spirit in my heart, my conscience can also say 'Amen!'

"Father, I desire to walk before you today with a good and clear conscience, and to do nothing that might grieve you or the Lord Jesus. I ask you that the power of the Holy Spirit, and the cleansing of the blood of Jesus be a living, continual, and effective deliverance in me from the power of sin, binding and strengthening me to your perfect will and service. And may my whole walk with you be in the joy of the united witness of my conscience and your Spirit, that I am well pleasing to you. Amen!"

CHAPTER 22

THE REVELATION OF THE SPIRIT

And my speech and my preaching were not with persuasive words of human wisdom, but in demonstration of the Spirit and of power, that your faith should not be in the wisdom of men but in the power of God. However, we speak wisdom among those who are mature, yet not the wisdom of this age, nor of the rulers of this age, who are coming to nothing. But we speak the wisdom of God in a mystery, the hidden wisdom which God ordained before the ages for our glory, which none of the rulers of this age knew... But God has revealed them to us through His Spirit... Now we have received, not the spirit of the world, but the Spirit who is from God, that we might know the things that have been freely given to us by God. These things we also speak, not in words which man's wisdom teaches but which the Holy Spirit teaches... But the natural man does not receive the things of the Spirit of God, for they

*are foolishness to him... But he who is spiritual judges all
things... 1 Corinthians 2:4-15*

There is a great contradiction between the spirit of
the world and the Spirit of God. It is most evidently
revealed in the wisdom or knowledge of the truth. It
was in the seeking of knowledge apart from God that man fell, and
it was in the pride of knowledge that godlessness had its origin.
Professing themselves to be wise, they became fools. (Romans 1:22). The
Greeks searched for truth, and sought their glory in wisdom and
philosophy. The Jews made their boast in the knowledge of God's
will, having *the form of the knowledge and of the truth in the law*
(see Romans 2:17-20). And yet when Christ, who *is* the wisdom of
God, (1 Corinthians 1:24), appeared on the earth, both Jews and
Greeks alike rejected him. Man's wisdom, even if it comes from a
revelation, is completely insufficient for comprehending God and
his wisdom. Just as man's heart is so alienated from God that he
does not love him or do his will, his mind is also darkened to the
extent that he cannot know God rightly. Even when the light and
the love of God shined down upon men in Christ, they did not
know it, or see its beauty.

In Paul's letter to the Romans, he addressed the issue of man's
trust in his own righteousness, and its total insufficiency. And in his
first letter to the Corinthians, especially in the first three chapters,
he exposes the complete insufficiency of man's wisdom. Not only
as when it was a question of discovering God's truth and will, as
with the Greeks, but even where God had revealed it, as with the
Jews, man was still incapable of seeing it without divine illumination - the light of the Holy Spirit. The rulers of this world, both
Jews and Gentiles, crucified the Lord of Glory because they did
not have, or know the wisdom of God. Paul warned the believers at
Corinth against the wisdom of this world. He was not addressing
heresy, but speaking to believers who had fully accepted his gospel
of a crucified Christ, yet were dealing with it in the power of their
human wisdom. He reminded them that the truth of God is a
hidden spiritual mystery, and can only be understood by spiritual

revelation. The rejection of Christ by the Jews was the greatest evidence of man's total incapacity to grasp divine revelation, apart from the internal spiritual revelation of the Holy Spirit.

The Jews prided themselves on their attachment to God's word and the law, and their study of it, and their conformity to it in their lives and conduct. However, they completely misunderstood it, and without being conscious of it, they ended up rejecting the very Messiah that they were waiting and hoping for. As Paul reveals in 1 Corinthians 2, divine revelation means three things: *1.) God makes known in his word what he thinks and does; 2.) Everyone who believes that they are called to communicate the message of God must not only be in possession of the truth, but they must also be taught by the Holy Spirit how to speak it; 3.) Finally, every hearer needs the inward illumination of the truth - it is only as the hearer is a spiritual man, with his or her life under the rule of the Spirit, that their minds can then take in spiritual truth.* Only as we have the mind and nature of Christ within us, can we rightly discern the truth as it is *in* Christ.

This teaching is what the entire body of Christ, and every believer needs today. Since the reformation, the insufficiency of man's own righteousness, and his power, or ability to fulfill God's law, has been recognized and accepted throughout most of the Church. However, the limitations and insufficiency of man's wisdom has not been as clearly understood. While the need for the Holy Spirit's teaching is generally admitted, we find that neither in our corporate messages, or in the lives of believers do these spiritual truths have any practical application or power. And without it, the wisdom and the spirit of this present world will continue to assert its influence and power over us.

The proof of what we have said can be found in what Paul said about his own preaching - *Our preaching was not in man's wisdom, but in the Spirit, that your faith might not rest in the wisdom of men, but in the power of God.* He is not writing of two gospels, as he did to the Galatians, but of two ways of proclaiming the one gospel of Christ. To preach the gospel in the persuasive words of man's wisdom, will only produce a faith that bears the mark of man's wisdom. It may stand as long as it is nourished and reinforced by men, but it cannot stand alone, or in the day of trial. Someone may become a believer through such preaching, but they will be a weak one. On the other hand, the faith that is born out of the preaching of the gospel in the Spirit and with the power of God, will stand alone and in the trials of life. That person is led by the preaching through the Holy Spirit himself, past all human understanding, into direct contact with the living God himself. And that person's faith will stand in the power of God alone. As long as the great majority of believers are in a weak and feeble state, with little of the faith that stands in the power of God, we can only conclude that it is due to our messages today, both spoken and written, which reflect more of the wisdom of men than the demonstration of the Spirit and power. If a change is to come, both in the spirit in which the messengers speak and write, and in which the listeners receive and understand, it must begin in the personal life of the individual believer.

We must learn to fear our own wisdom! *Trust in the Lord with all your heart, and lean not on your own understanding.* (Proverbs 3:5). Paul says, *If any man thinks he is wise, let him become a fool, that he may be wise.* (1 Corinthians 3:18). When scripture tells us that *they that are Christ's have crucified the flesh,* this includes the understanding of the natural, or fleshly mind. In the crucifixion of self I give up my own goodness, strength, and will unto death, because there is no good in it. I then turn to Christ by the power of his life *in me* to give me the goodness, strength, and will that is pleasing to God. While the wisdom of man is one of his noblest and most Godlike attributes, in his fallen state, sin rules in and over it. A man may be truly converted, and yet not fully understand to what extent that it is with his natural mind that he is attempting to grasp and hold onto the truth of God. The reason that there is so much bible teaching and reading today, which remains powerless alone to change or sanctify the life, is that it is not truth which has been revealed and received through the Holy Spirit.

This also applies to truth taught to us by the Holy Spirit, but after having been placed in our understanding, now only remains there by memory. Manna quickly loses its heavenly life when it is stored up on the earth. Truth received from heaven loses its divine freshness unless it is anointed with fresh oil each day. The believer needs to understand that there is nothing more insidious than the power of the natural mind of man in its dealing with the divine word of God. This revelation will help him believe that he must continually seek to 'become a fool.' Each time he touches God's word, or thinks of God's truth, he needs to wait in faith for the promised teaching of the Holy Spirit. He or she needs to ask for ears to hear, in which the power of their natural understanding has been removed, and the Spirit of the life of Christ within them listens in obedience, as Jesus did. To these the word will be fulfilled - "*I thank You, Father, that You have hidden these things from the wise and prudent, and have revealed them unto babes.*" (Matthew 11:25).

This lesson is for all apostolic leaders, prophets, evangelist, pastors, preachers, teachers, ministers, writers, theologians, students and readers of the bible, and should be regarded with fear and trembling. Do we understand yet that there must always be a perfect harmony between the objective spiritual content of a revelation, and the subjective spiritual understanding of it on our part? And then, between our understanding of it, and our communication of it, that both must be in the power of the Holy Spirit? And how about between our communicating of it and the receiving of it by those we bring it to? I pray that there would be written over all of our schools of ministry, bible colleges, seminaries, schools of theology, and over all the studies of our writers and commentators, our pastors, teachers, ministers, prophets and leaders, these words of Paul, *No one knows the things of God, except the Spirit of God... But God has revealed them unto us through his Spirit.* I pray that our leaders would influence and train the people under their care to see that it is not the amount of bible knowledge, or the degree of interest in it that will decide the extent of the blessing and power that is received, but it is the measure of one's complete dependance upon the Holy Spirit that determines real breakthrough. *Them that honor Me, I will honor.* No where will this word be found to be more true than here. The crucifixion of the self-life and all its wisdom - and the coming to God in weakness, with fear and trembling, as Paul did - will most certainly be met from above with the demonstration of the Spirit and of power.

Believer! It is not enough that the light of Christ shines *on* you in the word of God - the light of the Spirit must also shine *in* you. Each time you come to the word in study, or a message, or in the reading of a spiritual book, (yes, even this book), there should be a definite act of self-denial of your own wisdom, and a yielding of yourself in faith to your only divine teacher, the Holy Spirit. Believe with great assurance that he dwells within you. He seeks to conquer you, and to sanctify your inner life, in complete surrender and obedience to Jesus. Rejoice in renewing your full surrender to him. Reject the spirit of the world which is still in you, with all of its wisdom and self-confidence. Come in the poverty of your own spirit, to be led by the Spirit of God. *Be not conformed to the world* - with its confidence in itself and its own wisdom - *but be transformed by the renewing of your mind, that you may prove what is the good, and perfect, and acceptable will of God.* (See Romans 12:1-2). It is a transformed and renewed life alone - one that only wants to know God's perfect will - that will be taught by the Spirit. Cease from your own wisdom! Wait for the wisdom in your inner man that God has promised to you, and you will increasingly be able to testify of the things which have not entered, or even been conceived, into the hearts of men... *but God has revealed them to us by His Spirit.*

PRAYER:

"Oh God, I bless you for the wondrous revelation of yourself in the crucified Christ, who is the wisdom of God, and the power of God. I bless you, that while man's wisdom leaves him helpless in the presence of the power of sin and death, Jesus Christ crucified proves that he is the wisdom of God and the power of God. And I bless you Father, that what he worked in us, and grants to us, is revealed within us by the divine light of your Holy Spirit.

142

"Lord God, I ask you to teach all believers everywhere, that wherever Christ, as the power of God is not manifested, it is because Christ as the wisdom of God is so little known. I pray that the light of the indwelling Spirit alone would reveal him. May your leaders be taught to lead each child of God to the personal teaching and revelation of Christ within.

"Show us, Oh Lord, that our greatest hindrance to understanding the word and the truth of God is our own wisdom and imagination. Teach us to become fools in our own sight, that we might become wise in Christ. May our whole life become one continued act of faith, that the Holy Spirit will surely do his work of teaching, guiding and leading us into all truth. Father, you gave the Spirit to us so that he might reveal Jesus in all his glory within us. We wait for him! Amen."

CHAPTER 23

SPIRITUAL OR CARNAL

And I, brethren, could not speak to you as to spiritual people but as to carnal, as to babes in Christ. I fed you with milk and not with solid food; for until now you were not able to receive it, and even now you are still not able; for you are still carnal. For where there are envy, strife, and divisions among you, are you not carnal and behaving like mere men? 1 Corinthians 3:1-3

If we live in the Spirit, let us also walk in the Spirit. Galatians 5:25

In the previous chapter we saw how Paul contrasted the believer as a spiritual man, to the unregenerate as the natural, or soulish man - the man of the spirit, as opposed to the man of the soul. (See 1 Corinthians 2: 14-15). He said to the Corinthians, even though they had the Spirit, he could not call them spiritual. That title only belongs to those who have received the Spirit, and have also yielded themselves to him to possess and rule their entire life. Those who have not done this, whose lives still reflect the power and rule of the flesh (or the natural man), cannot be called spiritual - they are carnal, and of the flesh. There are therefore three states in which man may be found. *1.) The unregenerate is still the natural man, not having the Spirit of God. 2.) The regenerate, who are still babies in Christ - either because they are only recently converted, or they have stood still and have not grown in the faith - are still carnal, and still yield to the power of their flesh. 3.) Finally there is the believer in whom the Spirit has obtained full control and possession - that one is the true spiritual man or woman.* The passages above point to the rich instruction of the Holy Spirit regarding his life within us.

While regeneration is a new birth, the young Christian is still carnal. The root and center of the personality, which is the spirit of man, has been renewed and taken possession of by the Holy Spirit. But time is needed for the power of the Spirit flowing out from that center to extend throughout all of the parts and pieces of their lives. The kingdom of God is like a seed, and the life in Christ is a growth. It would be against the laws of grace and nature if we expected the baby in Christ to have the strength and maturity, and the rich experience that can only be found in an adult. Even in a young believer, where there is great singleness of heart and faith, with a true love and devotion to the Lord Jesus, time is still needed for them to experience a deeper knowledge of self and sin, and for a spiritual understanding into what God's will and grace are. With the new in Christ, it is not uncommon for their feelings and emotions to become deeply stirred, and their minds greatly stimulated as they contemplate their new life. However, as they grow in grace, the issue of their self-life and natural mind will determine the extent of their growth. If they can learn to wait for the Spirit's power in their life and character, they will experience greater joy than in those thoughts and images which the natural mind might give.

Many Christians remain in this carnal state and do not grow. God has not only called us to grow, but he has provided us with all of the conditions and power which are needed for growth. It is sad, but true, that there are many Christians today, just like the Corinthians, who have remained babes in Christ when they should be growing up into perfection, attaining to the stature of the fullness of Christ. (See Ephesians 4:13). The blame for this lies mostly with the Church and its messages, rather than the individuals themselves. When preaching or teaching is limited primarily to the salvation message of redemption, with its peace and hope of heaven, there will be limited growth. If holiness is preached, yet Christ as our source of power to be holy and sanctified, through the Spirit's indwelling, is not clearly taught, then growth can hardly be expected. Ignorance of the power of God for our present salvation, through sanctification, is the cause of this great error.

In other instances, the root of the error can be found in the unwillingness of the believer to deny themselves and crucify their flesh. The call of Jesus to every disciple is "*If any man will come after Me, let him deny himself.*" The Spirit is only given to the obedient. He can only do his work in those who are willing to absolutely give up their self-life unto death.

The sin that exposed the Corinthians as carnal was their jealousy and strife. When believers are not willing to give up the sin of selfishness and temper; when they want to keep their freedom to pronounce their own opinions and judgements; when they excuse their own ungodly thoughts and feelings, and behaviors, then they definitely will remain carnal. Regardless of all their *spiritual* knowledge, or their love of church life and worship, or even their work for the kingdom, they are still carnal, not spiritual, and they grieve the Holy Spirit. They cannot have the testimony that they are pleasing to God. *God is love.* If we do not love, then we are carnal. *Above all these things, put on love, which is the bond of perfection.* (Colossians 3:14).

The carnal Christian cannot comprehend spiritual truth. Paul said to the Corinthians, *I fed you with milk, and not with solid food; for you were not able to receive it, and even now you are still not able.* (1 Corinthians 3:2). The Corinthians prided themselves on their wisdom. Paul even thanked God that they were *enriched in all knowledge.* There was nothing in his teaching that they should not have been able to understand. But the real spiritual door to enter into the truth in power, to possess it and be possessed by it - to not only have the thoughts, but the very thing the words speak of - *comes only as the Holy Spirit gives it,* and he only gives it to the spiritually minded man or woman. The teaching and the leading of the Spirit is only given to the obedient believer, and is preceded by their being conquered by the Spirit in putting to death the deeds of the body (flesh). (See Romans 8:13-14). Spiritual knowledge is not deep thought, but a living experience, a union with truth as it is in Christ Jesus. It is a spiritual reality of an extraordinary existence. *The Spirit teaches, combining spiritual things with spiritual;* it is into a spiritual mind that he works spiritual truth. It is not the power of the intellect, or even the earnest desire to know the truth that prepares a believer for the Spirit's teaching. It is only a life that is yielded to him in waiting, with full dependence, total willingness, and complete obedience to be made spiritual, that will receive spiritual wisdom and understanding. In the scriptural meaning of the word *mind,* the moral and the intellectual elements are united. It is only as the former has precedence and influence can the latter understand what God has spoken.

It is easy to understand how a carnal or fleshly life, with its walk, and the fleshly mind, with its natural knowledge, act and react with one another. As long as we are submitted to the natural man within us, we are incapable of receiving spiritual understanding into truth. We may *know all mysteries, and have all knowledge,* but without love - the love that only the Spirit can work in the inner man - it is only a knowledge that puffs up, it profits nothing. The carnal/natural life turns the knowledge carnal, or natural. And this knowledge, being held in the natural mind, strengthens the religion of the fleshly/natural man, which centers on self-trust and self-effort; the truth received of God has no power to renew and set free. Again, there is no wonder that there is so much bible teaching and bible knowledge, yet with very little real spiritual results that lead to a life of holiness. I pray that God would reveal this word throughout his Church. *Where there is envy, jealousy, and strife among you, are you not still carnal?* Unless we are living spiritual lives, full of humility, love, and self-sacrifice, then the spiritual truth of God cannot enter, or profit us. Love alone is light - the lack of love is complete darkness. (See 1 John 2:9).

Every believer is called of God to be a spiritual man. Paul challenged these Corinthian believers, only a few short years after they had been brought out of complete darkness, that they were not yet spiritual. The primary objective of Christ's great redemption is the removal of every hindrance so that the Holy Spirit might make a believer's heart and life a worthy home and dwelling place for God himself. And that redemption was not a failure. The Holy Spirit came down to inaugurate a new and previously unknown era of God's indwelling life and power. The promise and the love of the Father, the power and the glory of the Son, and the presence of the Holy Spirit on earth, are all the pledge and guarantee that it is so. As sure as a natural man can be changed into a regenerated man, so also can a carnal/regenerate man become spiritual.

But why is this not so with so many believers? This question brings us face-to-face with a strange and hard to understand mystery: the choice that God has given to mankind to accept or refuse his offers, to be faithful, or unfaithful to the grace he has given. We have already pointed out the failure of the Church in her overall flawed teachings on the indwelling and sanctifying power of the Holy Spirit in the life of the believer. But the believer is also at fault for his or her unwillingness to fully surrender their lives to the Holy Spirit. It is only as the Spirit has the entire possession *of* them that he can do a perfect work *in* them. Again, let us try to understand what the scriptures teach as the way to become spiritual.

It is only the Holy Spirit who makes someone spiritual. He alone can do it, and he alone does it when someone's whole life is yielded to him. The sign of a spiritual one is that their whole being has been invaded, influenced, conquered, and sanctified by the Holy Spirit. This begins in the spirit, then moves to the soul - the mind, will, and emotions - and finally, even the body is brought under the Spirit's guidance and control.

The only way to achieve this is through faith. We must seek the deep and absolute, and totally absorbing conviction that the Holy Spirit is *in* us. He is the power of God that dwells and works in us. He is also the full representation of the Lord Jesus Christ in us, and makes him present in us as our Redeemer King, the one who saves. With fear and trembling at this revelation of an indwelling God, and with joy and trust in knowing him as our helper, (see John 16:7) - who brings in the irrevocable presence of the Father and the Son - this thought must become the inspiration of our lives: the Holy Spirit has his home within us; within our spirit is his hidden and holy dwelling place.

If we are filled with the faith of what he is and what he will do, and yet we do not see it fulfilled, we must ask him to reveal and expose any hidden sin or hindrances. Then we will see that there is still a power that opposes us - the flesh. From scripture we learn that our flesh is both unrighteousness and self-righteousness. Both must be confessed and surrendered into Jesus, whom the Holy Spirit has placed on the throne of our heart as Lord. Everything that is carnal, natural, or sinful, all the works of the flesh and the self-life must be given up and surrendered. Everything that is natural must be rooted out, even if it seems to be godly, righteous or good. Any confidence that we have in the flesh, all self-effort, and self-striving must go. The soul, with all of its carnal power, must be brought into full captivity and subjection to the Lord Jesus Christ. In total dependence on God, the Holy Spirit must be accepted, waited for, and followed each day.

If we walk in faith and obedience, we can be confident that the Holy Spirit will do a deep work within us. *If we live by the Spirit...* this is the faith that is needed to believe that the Holy Spirit dwells in us, and if that is true, then follows, *by the Spirit let us live.* This is the obedience that is asked. In the faith of the Holy Spirit, who is the Spirit of Christ in us, we know that we have the strength to walk by the Spirit and yield ourselves to his mighty working, to work out in us to will and to do all that is pleasing in God's sight. (See Ephesians 2:10).

PRAYER:

"Father, we humbly pray that you would fill us with holy fear and trembling so that even with our knowledge of the truth of Christ and the Holy Spirit, we would not be carnal or fleshly in our attitude and conduct, failing to walk in the love and the purity of your Spirit. May we understand that knowledge by itself only puffs up, unless it is brought under the rule of the love that builds up.

"Oh God, give us ears to hear your call to all your children to be spiritual! It is your purpose for us that even as with your beloved Son, our entire daily life, even in the least of things, would give evidence of bearing the fruit of your Spirit's indwelling. May we all accept the call, as from your life, that invites us to our highest blessing, that we would be conformed to the image and likeness of the Lord Jesus Christ within us. O God, by the power of your Spirit in us, help us become spiritual and not carnal. In Jesus we pray. Amen!"

CHAPTER 24

THE TEMPLE OF THE HOLY SPIRIT

Do you not know that you are the temple of God, and that the Spirit of God dwells in you? 1 Corinthians 3:16

The scriptures use the Temple of God as an analogy of God's dwelling in us by the Holy Spirit. The Temple was made according to the pattern that Moses saw on the mountain; it was a shadow of the eternal spiritual realities which it was to represent. Divine truth is exceedingly rich and full, and has many very diverse applications. One of these realities that was represented in the Temple is man's three-fold nature. Because man was created in the very image of God, the Temple is not only the revealing of the mystery of man's approach into the presence of God, but equally of God's way of entering into man in order to establish his dwelling place with him.

We are familiar with the division of the Temple into its three parts. First was the exterior, the Outer Court, seen by all men, which every Israelite could enter, and where all the external religious services were performed. Next was the Holy Place, which only the priest could enter, to present to God the blood or the incense, and the bread or the oil. Even though they were near in the Holy Place, they were still not within the veil; they were not able to come into the intimate and holy presence of God himself. God dwelt in the Holiest of All, (or The Holy of Holies), in an inaccessible light, where no one could come close. Only the High Priest could enter that place, and then only once a year. This established the absolute truth that until the veil was torn and taken away, there was no place for man to dwell in the presence of God.

But now *man* is God's Temple, and in him there are three parts as well. The body of man is like the *Outer Court,* external and visible, and regulated by God's law. It is man's body that interacts with all things around him, to protect him, and to bring him close to God. Next, there is the soul, with its inner life and its power of the mind, feelings, and will. In the man who is born of God, this is the *Holy Place,* where thoughts, affections, feelings, and desires move back and forth, like the priest of the sanctuary, and in the light of true consciousness, offers God his service. Finally, there is within the veil, in the spirit of man, concealed from all human sight and light, the hidden inner-most place, the Secret Place of the Most High, *The Holiest of All,* where God himself dwells, and where man may not enter until the veil is torn away by God himself. Man is not only body and soul, but also spirit. Deeper still than where the soul with its consciousness can enter, there is a spirit-nature linking man with God. So great is the power of sin that in some this place dies - they are sensual, but do not have the Spirit. In others, it is nothing more than a dormant power, a possibility waiting to come to life through the Holy Spirit. In the believer, it is the inner chamber of the heart, which the Spirit has taken possession of, and out of which he waits to do his glorious work of making the soul and body holy unto the Lord.

However, the indwelling of the Holy Spirit brings very little blessing unless it is recognized, and yielded to, and humbly maintained in faith. The one great lesson which the truth that we are God's Temple teaches us, is that we must actually acknowl-edge that God's holy presence dwells within us. This alone will enable us to regard the entire temple, even the Outer Court - our physical body - as sacred to God, and to surrender every power of our nature to his leading and will. The most sacred part of the Temple, which all the rest existed for and depended upon, was the Holiest of All. Even though the priest might never enter it, or see the glory that dwelt there, all of their conduct was regulated, and their faith was motivated by the thought of the unseen holy presence of God. This was what gave the sprinkling of the blood and the burning of incense their great value; it was what made it a privilege for them to draw near to God, and gave them confidence to go out and bless. It was the Holiest of All, the dwelling place of God's presence, that made the place of their serving holy. Their whole life was controlled and inspired by the faith of the unseen indwelling glory within the veil.

It is not any different with the believer. Until he learns by faith to tremble at the understanding of the wonderful mystery - God's Spirit dwells in him, therefore he is God's Temple - he will never fully and confidently yield himself to this high calling with the reverence and joy that he should. As long as he only looks into the Holy Place, into the heart as far as he is able to see or feel, he will often search in vain for the Holy Spirit, perhaps even encountering shame because he seems so lacking. Each of us must learn to know that there is within us, in our Temple, a Holiest of All. The Secret Place of the Most High within us must become the most important truth in our Temple worship. This must become the meaning of our confession: *I believe in the Holy Spirit.*

How do we make this deep faith in the hidden indwelling of the Spirit to become ours? We must stand firmly upon God's word and his promises, and believe that God truly means what he says in it. I am a Temple of God, and as much so as the Temple that he commanded to be built by Moses, David and Solomon. He means for me to understand what I am to become. In God's Temple, the Holiest of All - the innermost sanctuary - was the essential and central part. It remained hidden and dark, kept secret until the time it was unveiled. It demanded reverence and honor, and received the faith of the high priest and all the people. And the Holiest of All within me is also unseen and hidden, a thing for faith alone to know and encounter. As I approach the Holy One in reverence and honor, and declare unto him that I believe what he says, that his Holy Spirit - who is God, and is one with the Father and the Son - now has his dwelling place within me, I will meditate and be still before him, until something of the overwhelming glory of this truth falls upon me. Then faith in me will begin to realize that *I am* in fact his Temple, and in that secret place within his Temple *in me* he sits upon this throne. As I continue to yield myself to him each day, surrendering, and worshipping, and opening up my entire being to him, he will shine into my consciousness the full light of his loving presence and power.

As these divine thoughts fill my heart, the faith of his indwelling, though hidden presence, will influence me, and the Holy Place - my soul - will be ruled from The Holiest of All - my spirit. The world of consciousness in the soul, with all of its thoughts, feelings, affections and purposes, will surrender themselves to the holy power that sits within me on the throne. In the middle of the terrible experience of sin and failure, a new hope will arise. Even though I sought to keep the Holy Place - my soul - for God, I could not, because I did not know that he kept The Holiest of All for himself. If I give him the glory that he is due in my inner temple, he will send forth his light and truth throughout my whole being - my spirit, soul and body. Through my mind and will he will reveal his power which sanctifies and blesses. Then through the soul, which comes ever more fully under his rule, his power will be extended even into the body, with all of its passions and appetites. As my every thought is brought into complete captivity, the Holy Spirit within me will, through the soul, penetrate deeper and deeper into my body. Through the Spirit, the sinful actions of my body will be made powerless; then the river of living water which flows from under *the throne of God and the Lamb,* which is now within me, will pass through my body - which is the outer court - with its cleansing power.

Saints, believe that you are the Temple of the living God, and that the Spirit of God dwells in you! You have been sealed with the Holy Spirit, and he is the living assurance of your sonship, and of the Father's love. If you have had little comfort from this in the past, maybe this is the reason: you sought God in the Holy Place, your soul, among the thoughts, feelings, and experiences that you can see, but you could barely sense him there; you could not obtain the very comfort and strength that the Helper was meant to bring. No, you will not find him there. You must go deeper still, to the secret place of the Most High. Only there, deep *within you,* will you find him! Faith will find him there in your inner most part. And as faith worships in holy reverence before the Father, and the heart trembles at the thought of what it has found, wait in holy stillness for God to grant you the mighty working of his Spirit. Wait for the Holy Spirit, and be assured that, as he is God, he will arise and fill his Temple - you - with his glory.

Finally, remember that the veil was only for a time. When the preparation was complete, the veil of the flesh was torn in two. As you yield your soul's inner life to the inner most life of the Spirit, and as the flow between the Most Holy and The Holiest of All - your soul and your spirit - becomes more true and unbroken, fullness will come into your soul. In the power of Christ, in whom the veil was torn so that the Spirit might stream forth from his glorious body, there will come to you, as well, an experience in which the veil will be taken away, and the Most Holy, and The Holiest of All shall be one *within you!* The hidden glory of the secret place will stream into your conscious life daily, and the service of the Holy Place will all be in the power of the Holy Spirit.

Oh, let us fall down and worship! *Be silent all flesh, before the Lord, for He is awakened out of His holy habitation.* Zechariah 2:13.

PRAYER:

"Most Holy God, I bow before you in wonder and adoration of this glorious mystery of Grace: my whole spirit, soul and body is now your living Temple. In deep reverence and humility I

accept the holy revelation that there is in me a Holiest of All, just as there was in the Temple that the Israelites built, and that in the Holiest of All in me, your hidden glory dwells. Oh God, forgive me that I have known so little about it. I accept your truth that God the Spirit, the Holy Spirit, who is God Almighty, dwells in me! Please reveal to me what all that this means, lest I sin against you by saying it, but not living it.

"Blessed Lord Jesus, to you who sits upon the throne, I yield my whole spirit, soul and body. I trust you to rise up in power and have dominion within me, and over me. I believe in you for the full streaming forth of the living waters out of me.

"Blessed Holy Spirit, you are my holy teacher, my mighty sanctifier, and you are within me. I will wait upon you each and every day, all the day long. I belong to you. Please take entire possession of me, that the Father and the Son will come and dwell, and abide in me, and with me. Amen."

CHAPTER 25

THE MINISTRY OF THE SPIRIT

Not that we are sufficient of ourselves to think of anything as being from ourselves, but our sufficiency is from God, who also made us sufficient as ministers of the new covenant, not of the letter but of the Spirit; for the letter kills, but the Spirit gives life. But if the ministry of death... was glorious... how will the ministry of the Spirit not be more glorious? 2 Corinthians 3:5-8

In none of Paul's letters does he so clearly expound his revelation of ministry as he does in this second letter to the Corinthians. His need to defend his calling as an apostle against his detractors; his deep consciousness of the divine power and glory that was working in him - even in the midst of great weakness - and his intense longing to communicate from his heart all that he had to impart, were things that stirred him deeply. He presents the innermost secrets of the life that makes one a true minister of Christ and his Spirit. In our text we have this central thought: he finds his strength, and the inspiration and rule of all his conduct, in that he has been made a minister of the Holy Spirit.

If we take the different passages in which he mentions the Holy Spirit in the first half of this letter, we will see what he believes was the place and the work of the Holy Spirit in his own ministry, and what the characteristics are of a ministry that is under the Holy Spirit's leading and power.

In this letter Paul speaks with authority, and yet places himself on the same level as his readers. When he first mentions the Holy Spirit, he tells them that the Spirit that is in him is the same Spirit that lives in them. *Now He who establishes us with you in Christ and has anointed us is God, who also has sealed us and given us the Spirit in our hearts as a guarantee,* (2 Corinthians 1:21-22). **The work of the Holy Spirit is to anoint the believer with the Spirit, and bring him into fellowship and union with Christ himself.** The anointing reveals what he is to us, which is the earnest deposit of the Spirit, or his sealing, which marks us as his own. He secures for us a taste of heaven, and then prepares us for our glorious heavenly inheritance. Paul addresses all that was wrong and unholy among the Corinthians, but still thinks of them, and loves them as one with him in Christ. *He that establishes us with you in Christ, and anointed us...* This deep sense of unity fills his soul and emerges throughout the letter. It is the secret of his power. (See 2 Corinthians 1:6, 10; 2:3). He goes on, *My joy is the joy of you all,* (chapter 4:5); *ourselves your servants,* (chapter 4:10-12); *death works in us, life in you,* (4:15); *all things for your sakes,* (5:11); *you are in our hearts to live and die with you,* (7:3). If the unity of the Spirit - the consciousness of being members of one another - is necessary in all believers, how much more must it be the mark of those who minister? The power of the ministry to the saints depends upon the unity of the Spirit, and the full recognition of all believers as partakers of the anointing. To this end the minister must live as an anointed and sealed one by the Holy Spirit, revealing and demonstrating that he or she has the earnest deposit of the Spirit in their heart. (See 2 Corinthians 13:5).

In 2 Corinthians 3:3 Paul says, *You are an epistle of Christ, ministered by us, written not with ink, but by the Spirit of the living God, not on tablets of stone, but on tablets of flesh, that is, of the*

160

heart. The writing of the law on tablets of stone was a distinct act of God, and so too is the writing of the law of the Spirit, and the name of Christ, on the heart. It is a divine work, and as sure as God wrote the old, the Holy Spirit uses the tongue of his true minister as his pen. It is this truth that needs to be restored in the ministry today - not only that the Holy Spirit is needed, but that he waits, and when the right relationship with him is maintained, he is willing to do the work. Paul's own experience at Corinth (see Acts 18:5-11 and 1 Corinthians 2:3) teaches us that conscious weakness, fear and trembling, and an absolute helplessness are needed in order for the power of God to rest upon us. The entire letter of 2 Corinthians confirms this. Paul was a man under the sentence of death, bearing about the dying of the Lord Jesus in his flesh, so that the life and power of Christ could be revealed in him. (See 2 Corinthians 4:10). The Spirit of God stands in stark contrast to the world, the flesh, and the self, with its life and strength. When these are broken down, and the self-life has nothing left to glory in, then the Spirit will work. I pray that every minister, preacher, teacher, and writer's tongue might be prepared by the Holy Spirit to be used as a pen in which God writes on the hearts of all.

Then comes the words from 2 Corinthians 3, verses 6 and 7, to teach us what the special characteristic is of the new covenant ministry of the Spirit - *it gives life.* The antithesis to *the letter kills* applies not only to the law of the old covenant, but to all knowledge which is not in the *life giving* power of the Holy Spirit. We cannot emphasize this enough - even as the letter of the law was spiritual, so the gospel too has its letter. The gospel may be preached very clearly and faithfully; it may exert a strong moral influence, and yet the faith that comes forth out of it may stand in the wisdom of men, rather than in the power of God. If there is one thing that we need to pray for today, it is that the ministry of the Spirit is restored to us in his full power. Pray that God may teach us what it is to personally live in the anointing, the sealing power, and the assurance of the indwelling Spirit. Pray that we understand and know that the *letter kills*, but the *Spirit gives life.* And above all, pray that the personal life of every believer is under the ministry and authority of the Holy Spirit so that he is free to work through us.

Paul now proceeds to contrast the old of the letter and the newness of the Spirit, and the different characteristics of those who live in them. He declares that as long as the mind is blinded, there is a veil on the heart which can only be taken away as we turn to the Lord. Then he adds, *Now the Lord is the Spirit, and where the Spirit of the Lord is, there is liberty. But we all, with unveiled faces, beholding as in a mirror the glory of the Lord, are being transformed into the same image from glory to glory, just as from the Lord, [who is] the Spirit.* (2 Corinthians 3:17-18 NASB). It is because God *is the Spirit* that he can *give* the Spirit. It was when the Lord Jesus was exalted into the life of the Spirit that he became *the Lord, who is the Spirit,* who could give the Holy Spirit, and then in him come to his people himself. The disciples knew Jesus for a long time, yet they did not know him as *the Lord, who is the Spirit.* Paul speaks of this too, with regard to himself, (see 2 Corinthians 5:16). In the ministry today there is much sincere preaching of Jesus as the crucified one, without the preaching of him as the Lord, who is the Spirit. Only as this latter truth is taught, and understood, and experienced, can the blessing come that Paul speaks of here - *Where the Spirit of the Lord is, there is liberty* - and believers will be led into the glorious liberty of the children of God. (See Romans 8:2; Galatians 5:1, 18). Then he will do the work for which he was sent to do, which is to reveal the glory of the Lord in us. And as we behold his glory, we shall be changed from glory to ever increasing glory into his very image and likeness. Before Pentecost, it was written of Jesus, *The Spirit was not yet [given], because Jesus was not yet glorified.* (John 7:39). But when he had been *justified in the Spirit, and received up in glory,* (see 1 Timothy 3:16), the Spirit came forth from that excellent glory into our hearts, that we, with unveiled faces beholding the glory of the Lord, might be changed into his very likeness, from glory to ever increasing glory. What a calling! The ministry of the Holy Spirit is to hold up the glory of the Lord Jesus to his redeemed ones, to be used by his Spirit in working out their transformation into his very own likeness.

Therefore, seeing that we have this ministry, we do not lose heart, (2 Corinthians 4:1). It is as this knowledge and acknowledgment of Christ as the Lord, who is the Spirit, that through the Spirit, Christ himself changes believers into his very own likeness. He lives in the Church, which is his own body, that the ministry among believers will be in life and power, the ministry of the Spirit.

The power of the ministry on the divine side is the Spirit - on the human side it is faith. The next mention of the Spirit in 2 Corinthians 4:14 says, *having the same Spirit of faith.* After establishing the glory of the ministry of the Spirit and the gospel it preached, in 2 Corinthians chapter 3, and 4:1-6, Paul then turns to the vessels in which this glory dwells. He has to justify his own apparent weakness, but instead of apologizing for it, he expounds its divine meaning and glory. He proves how his circumstances reveal God's power, because only in his weakness could divine power work. It has been ordained *that the excellency of the power may be of God and not of us,* (see 2 Corinthians 4:7). Therefore, his perfect fellowship with Jesus was maintained as he bore about *the dying of the Lord Jesus, so that the life of Jesus might be revealed in his mortal body.* (4:10). There was even in Paul's suffering something of the element that marked his Lord's life - *So then death works in us, but life in you,* (4:12). He then adds, as the expression of the genuine power that sustained him through all his trials and labors, *But having the same Spirit of faith according to that which is written, I believed, and therefore I spoke - we also believed, and therefore we also speak; knowing that He who raised up the Lord Jesus shall also raise us up with Jesus and shall present us with you,* (4:13-14).

Faith is the evidence of things not seen. It *sees* the invisible, and lives in it. Beginning with trust in Jesus, *in whom, though you do not see Him, yet you believe, and you rejoice,* (1 Peter 1:8), it goes on throughout the entirety of the Christian life. Whatever is of the Spirit, is by faith. God's great work is to open the heart of his child to receive more of the Holy Spirit, to bring his faith into a greater freedom from what is seen, and into the complete rest in God, and to bring him into the complete confidence that God dwells and works powerfully within his child's own weakness.

This is the reason that trials and sufferings are sent. Paul uses some remarkable language regarding his own sufferings in 2 Corinthians 1:9, *Yes, we had the sentence of death in ourselves, that we would not trust in ourselves but in God, who raises the dead.* Even Paul was in danger of trusting in himself. There is nothing more natural. All life is confident of self, and nature is consistent with itself until it dies. For the great work that he was called to do, he needed to trust nothing less than the Living God, who raises the dead. God led Paul to this conclusion by giving him the afflictions and trials that came upon him in Asia, the sentence of death in himself. The trial of his faith was its strength. In our context he returns to this thought: the fellowship of the dying of Jesus is the means and the assurance of the experience of the power of Christ's life. In the spirit of this faith he speaks, *Knowing that He who raised up Jesus shall raise us up also,* (4:14).

It was not until Jesus had died that the Spirit of Life could break forth from him. The life of Jesus was born out of the grave - it is a life out of death. It is as we die daily and carry about in our own bodies the dying of Jesus - as flesh and blood are kept crucified and put to death; as we have in ourselves God's sentence of death on all that is of self and nature - that the life and the Spirit of Jesus will be manifested in us. This is the Spirit of faith, that in the midst of weakness and death, it relies only on God, who raises the dead. This is the ministry of the Spirit, when faith glorifies in infirmities and weakness, that the power of Christ may rest upon it. As our faith does not stagger at the enormity of our earthly weaknesses, as it consents to the fact that the excellency of the power that works within us is not from ourselves, but from God, then the Spirit will work in us in the power of the Living God.

We see the same thought in the two remaining passages of our text. In 2 Corinthians 5:5, Paul speaks of the *Spirit as a guarantee* in connection with our groanings and burdens. Then in chapter 6 in verses 4-10, in the middle of his listing all his distresses and labors, the Spirit is introduced as the very mark of his ministry. *But in all things we commend ourselves as ministers of God: in much patience, in tribulations, in needs, in distresses, in stripes... **in the***

Holy Spirit... as dying, and behold we live; as chastened, and yet not killed; as sorrowful, yet always rejoicing; as poor, yet making many rich; as having nothing, and yet possessing all things. The power of Christ in the Holy Spirit was to Paul such a living reality, that the weakness of his flesh only led him to rejoice and trust in him even more. The Holy Spirit's dwelling and working in him was the primary mark, and the power of his entire ministry.

We may ask, "Is the Holy Spirit willing to take the same place in our life and ministry as he did with Paul?" There is no one who is in ministry today in any capacity, or in the body of Christ, who believes in the Lord Jesus Christ, who is not interested in the answer to this question. ***The question is not whether we admit to our absolute need of the Holy Spirit's working, but whether or not we are willing to surrender our lives so completely that he will have his place in us as the Spirit of the Lord?*** Does the Holy Spirit have the place in our ministries and in the Church which the Lord Jesus desires for him to have? When our hearts open to the inconceivable and glorious truth that he is the mighty power of God dwelling in us, that in him the living Christ works through us, and that he is the real presence of the glorified Lord on the throne with us, we will feel that the one need of the ministry and the Church is this: to humble ourselves before him, and wait without ceasing to be clothed with his power. The Spirit of Christ, in his love and power, in his death and life, is the Spirit of the ministry. As we grasp this, it will be what the head of the Church, the Lord Jesus Christ himself, meant it to be - the ministry of the Spirit.

PRAYER:

"Father, we thank you for the ministry of the Lord Jesus through the Holy Spirit. We thank you that this ministry of the Spirit gives life to us through your word, and through his working out in us the life of Jesus in Spirit and in power.

"Grant us the wisdom to see how far we fall short of your purposes by seeking to do your works out of our own power. Expose us as to how much we rely on our own zeal, wisdom

and strength, which is of our self-life. Show us how to give ourselves up to the Lord Jesus, so that the Holy Spirit can change us into the vessels he desires to use. O God, give us the conscious presence of Christ to be in our hearts through the Holy Spirit, and give us great boldness of speech and actions. May his divine power in the midst of our weakness be the mark of our ministries.

"Teach us, Oh Lord, to wait upon the Holy Spirit for our teaching, and to receive it, and to submit to it as the ministry of the Spirit. May the lives of believers everywhere be increasingly lived out in the power of such a ministry. This is your Church led and sanctified by the Holy Spirit. Amen!"

CHAPTER 26

THE SPIRIT AND THE FLESH

Are you so foolish? Having begun in the Spirit, are you now being made perfect by the flesh? Galatians 3:3

For we are the circumcision, who worship God in the Spirit, rejoice in Christ Jesus, and have no confidence in the flesh, though I also might have confidence in the flesh. Philippians 3:3-4

The flesh is the name that scripture designates to our fallen nature - the soul and body. At creation the soul was positioned between the spiritual, (or divine), and the senses, (or worldly), to guide them into that perfect union, which would result in man attaining his true destiny: a spiritual body. When the soul yielded to the temptation of the senses, it broke away from the rule of the Spirit and came under the power of the body - it became flesh. And now the flesh is not only without the Spirit, but it is actually hostile towards it. *For the desires of the flesh are opposed to the [Holy] Spirit.* (Galatians 5:17 AMPC).

In this antagonism of the flesh towards the Spirit, there are two sides. On one hand, the flesh is now opposed to the Spirit, as it commits sin and transgresses God's law. And on the other, its hostility to the Spirit is equally strong as it seeks to serve God and do his will. In yielding to the flesh, the soul sought itself instead of the God to whom the Spirit had linked it to. Out of selfishness it overruled God's will, and selfishness became its ruling principle. Now man's spirit of self, the flesh, is so subtle and powerful that it not only sins against God, but even when the soul seeks to serve God, it still asserts its own power, and refuses to let the Spirit lead. In its efforts to be religious, it is still the great enemy that constantly hinders and quenches the Spirit. Because of this deceitfulness of the flesh, there often occurs what Paul speaks of to the Galatians - *Having begun in the Spirit, are you now being made perfect by the flesh?* Unless the surrender to the Spirit is complete, which is waiting on him in humility and total dependance, what began in the Spirit easily and quickly passes over to confidence in the flesh. Here is a paradox - as soon as the flesh seeks to serve God, it becomes the power of sin.

If you will recall, it was the Pharisees, with their self-righteousness and carnal religion, who fell into pride and selfishness, and became the servants of sin. And it was the Galatians that Paul pressed the question about perfecting in the flesh what they had begun in the Spirit. He strongly warned them against the righteousness of works, because the works of the flesh were so present among them that they were in danger of devouring one another. Satan has no more sinister means for keeping souls in bondage than to incite them to a religion in the flesh. He knows that the power of the flesh can never please God or conquer sin, and that in due time the flesh that has gained command over the Spirit in the service to God, will also assert and maintain that same authority in its service to sin. It is only where the Spirit has preeminence and the rule in the life of worship, that it will have the power to lead and rule in the life of practical obedience. If I am to deny self in my relationships with people, to conquer selfishness and temper, and overcome my lack of love, I must learn to first deny myself in my relationship to God. There the soul, the seat of self, must learn to bow down to the Spirit, where God dwells.

The contrast between worship in the Spirit and trusting in the flesh is expressed in Paul's description of the true circumcision, which is the circumcision of the heart, whose praise is not of men, but of God - *Who worship God in the Spirit, glorying in Christ Jesus, and have no confidence in the flesh,* (Galatians 3:3). By placing the glorying in Christ Jesus in the center, as the very essence of our faith and life, he points out on the one hand the great danger by which it is assaulted, and on the other the safeguard through which it is fully secured. Confidence in the flesh is the one thing above all else that renders the glorying in Christ to no effect. Worship by the Spirit is the only thing that makes it truly life and truth. May the Spirit reveal to us what it means to truly glory in Christ Jesus!

All of history teaches that there is a glorying in Christ Jesus that is accompanied by much confidence in the flesh. It was this way with the Galatians. The teachers whom Paul opposed so earnestly were all preachers of Christ and his cross. But they preached, not as men led and inspired by the Holy Spirit to know and understand what the infinite and all encompassing influence the cross must be, but as men who began in the Spirit, and then came to rely upon their own wisdom and understanding to define the cross, thereby reconciling it to a religion that was very legal and carnal. Sadly, the story of the Galatian Church is repeated often today in the churches that are the most confident that they are free from the 'Galatian error.' The doctrine of justification by faith is spoken of in this generation as if it were the only teaching of the epistle, while the teaching of the Spirit's indwelling by faith, and walking by the Spirit, is rarely mentioned.

Jesus Christ crucified is the wisdom of God. The confidence in the flesh, in connection with the glorying in Christ, is seen in the confidence of its own wisdom. The bible is studied and preached, and listened to and believed, but mostly in the power of the natural mind, with virtually no emphasis upon the absolute need for the Spirit's personal teaching. The word of God is seen in the complete confidence in which men seem to know that they have the truth - though what they actually have is more from human wisdom than divine teaching - which comes in the lack of the teachableness that waits for God himself to reveal his own truth in his own light by the Spirit.

Christ, through the Holy Spirit, is not only the wisdom of God, but he is also the power of God. (See 1 Corinthian 1:24). The confidence in the flesh is seen and felt in much of the work of the Church, where human effort and preparation are emphasized much more than waiting on the power that comes only from God. In larger Christian organizations, in individual churches and movements, and even in the inner life of the heart of most believers, most of their ineffective efforts and repeated failures can be traced back to this one sin. There is no lack of acknowledging Christ as our only hope, and there is no lack of giving him all the glory - yet there remains so much confidence in the flesh, which effectively renders it all as empty. Let me ask it here again - is it possible that there are many who are striving for a life in the fullness of consecration and blessing, who find this as the reason for their failure? My primary objective in writing this book, and my most earnest prayers, are to help them in this matter.

Many people have at times, through a message, a book, a conversation, or during private prayer, have found the fullness of Jesus opened up to them with the possibility of a holy life in him; the soul felt it so beautifully and so simply that nothing could keep them from it any longer. Perhaps they entered into a time of great enjoyment with the Lord, and they experienced a power that they had not previously known. It all gloried in Christ Jesus! But it did not last; there was a worm at its root. The soul searched in vain for what was the cause, or how they could be restored to what was. Often the only answer that could be found was that their surrender was not absolute, or their faith's acceptance was not complete. And yet their soul felt sure that it was ready to give it all up, that it did seek to let Jesus have everything and to trust him completely. The promise had been that it would all be so simple - just the sort of life for the poor and weak - and yet, failure! If perfect consecration and perfect faith were to be the conditions of the blessing, the soul could become nearly hopeless as it pursues an impossible perfection.

Listen to the teaching from the word of the Lord. It was *your* confidence in the flesh that spoiled your glorying in Christ Jesus. It was your *self* doing what only the Spirit can do. It was your *soul* that took the lead, in the hope that the Spirit would bless its efforts, instead of trusting and waiting on the Holy Spirit to lead and do it all. It was trying to follow Jesus, without denying yourself. This is the secret of most failure. Listen to Paul as he tells of the only safeguard from this danger: *For we are the circumcision, who worship God in the Spirit, rejoice in Christ Jesus, and have no confidence in the flesh,* (Philippians 3:3). Here are the two elements of spiritual worship - **1.) the Spirit exalts Christ, and 2.) the Spirit reduces the flesh.** If we would truly glory in Jesus, and have him glorified in us; if we would know the glory of Jesus in personal and unchanging experience, free from the failure which always marks the efforts of the flesh, we must simply learn what this worship of God is by the Spirit.

Again, the purpose of this book is to reveal God's truth from his word - **Glory in Christ Jesus; glory in him as the Glorified One who baptizes with the Holy Spirit.** In simplicity and trust believe in him as having given his own Spirit within you. Believe in his gift! Believe in the Holy Spirit dwelling within you. Accept this as the secret of the life of Christ in you. The Holy Spirit is dwelling in the hidden recesses of your spirit. Meditate on this! Believe Jesus and his words concerning it, until your soul bows with holy awe and fear before God under the glory of this truth - the Holy Spirit of God is indeed dwelling in me.

Yield yourself to his leading. We have learned that his leading is not just in our minds thoughts, or feelings, but it is in the *life* and *personality*. Yield yourself fully to God, to be guided by the Holy Spirit in all your conduct. He is promised to those who love Jesus and obey him. Do not be afraid to confess to him that he knows you love and obey him with your whole heart. Remember that the one central objective of the Spirit's coming was to restore the departed Lord Jesus to his disciples. *"I will not leave you as* orphans," said Jesus, "I will come again for you," (John 14:18). I cannot glory in a distant Jesus 'out there somewhere.' When I try to do it, it's a thing of effort and I have to have the help of my flesh to do it. I can only truly glory in a present, close, accessible savior, whom the Holy Spirit glorifies and reveals in all his glory *within* me. As he does this, the flesh is diminished, and is kept in its place of crucifixion as a cursed thing. And then the deeds of the flesh, with their control over me, are put to death. My only 'religion' is to have no confidence in the flesh, and to glory in Christ Jesus, and worship by the Spirit of God.

Dear friends, having begun in the Spirit, please continue, go on, persevere in the Spirit! Beware of trying to perfect the work of the Spirit through your flesh, not even for a moment! Let the words *"I have no confidence in the flesh"* be your battle cry. Let a deep distrust of the flesh, and a great fear of grieving the Holy Spirit by walking after the flesh, keep you humble before God. Pray to God for the spirit of revelation that you may see how Jesus is all and does all, and how by the Holy Spirit a divine life takes the place of your life, and Jesus is enthroned as the keeper and guide, and the life of your soul.

PRAYER:

"Blessed Father, we thank you for the wondrous provision that you have made for your children to draw close to you, and to glory in the Lord Jesus Christ, and worship by the Spirit. We pray that this would be our life, and that we would constantly grow closer to you, by the Spirit.

"Continue to show us, we pray, how our one great hindrance to a life in Christ, is the power of our flesh and all the efforts of our self-life. Open our eyes, Lord, to this snare from Satan. May we see clearly the secret and sinister temptations for us to place our confidence in the flesh, after we began this new life in the Spirit. May we learn to trust you to work in us by your Spirit, both in our will and obedience.

"Teach us, Father, we pray, to know how our flesh can be conquered and all its power broken. In the death of Jesus our old nature has been crucified. May we count all this as loss so that we are fully conformed to his death, so that the old nature is kept in its place. And may we walk in the newness of life by your Spirit. We yield ourselves to be led and ruled by your Spirit. We believe and confess through the Spirit that the Lord Jesus Christ is our life, so that instead of the life of effort and work by the flesh, we now live a new life that works within us, a life by the Spirit. Father, in faith we give up our all to your Spirit to be the life of our life. Amen!"

CHAPTER 27

THE SPIRIT THROUGH FAITH

Christ has redeemed us from the curse of the law... that the blessing of Abraham might come upon the Gentiles in Christ Jesus, that we might receive the promise of the Spirit through faith. Galatians 3:13-14

The word faith is used for the first time in scripture with Abraham. His highest praise and the secret of his strength for obedience was that he *believed* God. He pleased God so much that he became the father of all them that believe. His was the great example of this blessing which divine favor gives, and the way in which it comes. Just as God proved himself to Abraham as the God who gives life to the dead, he also does to us in even greater measure, by giving us his own Spirit to live in us as his own life. As this life giving power came to Abraham through faith, now the same blessing that Abraham received, which is the promise of the Spirit revealed in Christ, is made ours by faith. All of the lessons of Abraham's life are centered on this: *we receive the promise of the Spirit through faith.* If we desire to know the faith through which the Spirit is received, and how it comes and grows, we need to study the life of Abraham.

With Abraham we see that *faith* is the spiritual sense in which man recognizes and accepts the revelation of God, and the divine belief that is called forth and awakened by that revelation. It was because God chose to reveal himself that Abraham became a man of faith. Each new revelation was a function of God's will. And the revelation of God's will and his purposes is the motivation and the power of a life of faith. The more distinct the revelation of God, the deeper faith is stirred in the soul. Paul said, *Trust in the Living God.* As he draws near and touches the soul with the power of the divine life, *faith* is called forth. Faith is not our independent response to what God says, and it is not merely a passive state, where we allow God to do whatever he wills. As God comes near and speaks to us and touches us with his living power, faith is the soul's ability to receive and accept him, and yield fully to his words and ways.

It is evident that faith has two things to address - the presence of God, and the word of God. It is his living presence that makes the living word; the kingdom comes not only in word, but also in power. It is because of this that there is so much teaching, reading, and preaching of the word of God that bears very little fruit. And there is much praying and straining for faith, with so little results. Believers interact with the word of God more than the God of the word. Faith has been defined as *taking God at his word.* To many this means *taking the word as God's.* They don't see the power of the thought, *taking God* at his word. A door knob has no value or use unless it is used to open the door. Likewise it is only in our direct contact with the Living God that the word of God will open the heart to believe. Faith takes God at his word - it can only do this when he gives himself - he must inhabit his own word. I may have all of his precious promises in my bible, and I may fully understand that I only need to trust in these promises to have them fulfilled, and yet I continue to fail to see them come to pass. The faith that enters into the inheritance is the attitude of my soul, which waits for God himself, first to speak his word to me, and then to do the thing he has spoken. Faith is true fellowship with

God. It is surrender to him; it is the impression he makes when he draws near; it is the possession of my soul that he takes through his word, holding it and preparing it for his work. Once faith has been awakened within us, it watches for every indication of his divine presence, and every appearance of his divine will. Then it will look for, and expect the fulfillment of all his promises.

This was the faith in which Abraham inherited the promises that God made to him. And it is the same faith through which the blessing of Abraham, the promised Holy Spirit, comes upon all believers in Christ. In our study of the Spirit and the way in which he comes - from his first sealing us, to his full indwelling and streaming forth from us - let us hold fast to this word, *we receive the promise of the Spirit through faith.* Regardless of what you are seeking, whether it is the full consciousness of the Spirit's indwelling, or greater assurance of God's love, or more fruit, truth, or power for your work, let us remember that the law of faith on which God's grace is based upon, demands its fullest application - *According to your faith be it unto you.* We receive the promise of the Spirit by faith. Let us seek Abraham's promise in Abraham's faith.

Our faith must begin where Abraham's faith began - in meeting with, and waiting on God. *The Lord appeared unto Abraham... and Abraham fell on his face... and God talked with him.* Let us look to the God, who wants to fill us with his Spirit and his power. The blessing that he has for us is the same one that he gave Abraham, only more wonderful. To Abraham, when he was old and as good as dead, and later, when his son Isaac was lying on the alter, bound and waiting for death, God came as the *life giver - He believed God, who gives life to the dead... Abraham offered up Isaac, accounting that God was able to raise him up.* To us he comes and offers to fill our whole spirit, soul and body, through the Holy Spirit dwelling within us, with the power of his divine life. Let us be like Abraham, who, while looking at God's promise to him, did not waver through unbelief, but remained strong through faith, and became fully assured that what *God had promised, he was also able to perform.* Let our souls be filled with the God of faith, who has promised, and let our hearts be focused only on God, who is able to perform. It is faith *in* God that opens the heart *for* God, and then prepares it to submit *to* God. He waits on us to fill us with his Spirit; let us wait on him to be filled. He is the one who acts - wait on him. It is okay to long for, and pray, to dedicate ourselves to grasping the promise, to believe and hold fast to the truth that the Spirit dwells within us; but these, while good in their place, do not bring, in themselves, the promise. The one thing needed is that our hearts are filled with *FAITH* in the Living God, and in that faith we abide with him in living fellowship, waiting, worshipping and working in his presence. This is the fellowship with God where the Holy Spirit fills our hearts.

Once we take this position, let us stay in it; we are in the place where the Spirit will reveal more of what God has prepared for us. As we meditate on the revelations of the Holy Spirit regarding the promises in God's word of the life of the Spirit in us, we will remain in humble dependance upon him where childlike trust can emerge. We can then be protected from a life of strain and effort, which so often leads to failure. Too many times in our attempts to serve God in the Spirit, the trust and confidence in what we felt, or did, or wanted to do, was always in the flesh. The deep undertone of our life - either in listening, or asking, in meditation or worship, or in ministry or daily life - will be the assurance that overpowers every other certainty: "*How much more will the Heavenly Father give...*" - has given, and will alway be giving - "*the Holy Spirit to them that ask him.*" (See Luke 11:13).

There will be trials that accompany this level of faith. Isaac, who was the very promise from God, had to be given up to death, so that he might be received back as a life raised from the dead. And the God-given experience of the Holy Spirit's work in us, may at times slip away, leaving the soul dull and dead. This will last until the lessons of faith have been fully learned. They are, *first,* that the living faith can only rejoice in a living God, even when all feelings and experiences contradict the promise. And, *second,* the divine life enters our life *only* as the life of the flesh is given over to death. The *life* of Christ is revealed in us as his *death* works in us, and we look to him in our weakness. *We receive the promise of the Spirit through faith.* Nothing else! As faith grows larger and broader, the promise of the Spirit will be received deeper and fuller. With each new revelation of God to Abraham, his faith becomes stronger, and his relationship with God became more intimate. When God drew near, Abraham knew what to expect; he knew he could trust him in even the most difficult of commands, such as when God asked for the death of Abraham's son of promise. This is the faith that waits every day on God to reveal himself; this is the faith that grows with ears to hear, and obedience, and yields fully to his presence. This is the faith that knows that only as God wills to reveal himself, can the promised blessing come; but because he loves to reveal himself, we can trust it will surely come. This is the faith that receives the promise of the Spirit.

It was in God's presence that this faith was awakened and strengthened in Abraham, and in the saints of old. It was in Jesus's presence on earth that unbelief was cast out, and weak faith became strong; it was in his presence that faith received the blessing of Pentecost. The throne of God is now open to us in Christ; it is now the throne of God and the Lamb. As we wait before this new throne in humility, obedience, and true worship, the river of the water of life that flows out from under it will flow into us, and out through us. *"He that believes in Me, rivers of living water shall flow out of him."* (John 7:38).

PRAYER:

"Father, we pray that you would reveal yourself to us, as much as we can bear it. Increase in us, we pray, the faith that is needed to know you and receive your divine love and power. We seek your faith to receive all that you are to us. Please convince us that we have as much of your Spirit as we have faith.

"Lord, we know that it is your presence that works faith in the soul that is yielded to you. Draw us, we pray, ever closer to your holy presence, and keep us there. Please deliver us from our terrible fascination with the world and our flesh. We pray that your glory may be our all consuming desire, and that our

whole heart is emptied so that we can receive the Holy Spirit's revelation of the fullness of Christ within us. We desire to take your words and let them dwell in us richly. We desire for our soul to be silent before you, and that we would wait for you.

"Father, we want to fully trust and believe that you have given us your Spirit within us, and that the Spirit is now working in secret to reveal your Son fully to us. O God, we desire to live this life of faith, and we believe in the Holy Spirit! Amen!"

CHAPTER 28

WALKING IN THE SPIRIT

Walk in the Spirit, and you shall not fulfill the lust of the flesh. Those who are Christ's have crucified the flesh with its passions and desires. If we live in the Spirit, let us also walk in the Spirit. Galatians 5:16. 24-25

*I*f we live in the Spirit, let us also walk in the Spirit. These words suggest the clear difference between the sick and the healthy Christian life. The sick, or weak Christian, is content to *live by the Spirit* - he is satisfied with the *new life,* but does not *walk in the Spirit.* The healthy believer, however, is not content with anything less than living out his life in the power of the Holy Spirit. This believer *walks in the Spirit,* and does not fulfill the *lust of his flesh.*

As this one seeks to walk out his life pleasing to the Lord, he is often troubled by the power of sin in his life, and his failure to conquer it. He usually resolves that it is due to his own weakness, or lack of faith, or Satan's overwhelming power. But these may not be the cause at all. It would be better if he sought the Lord, his deliverer, for the buried reasons that sin and failure continue to overcome him. One of the deepest secrets of the Christian life, and the most powerful obstacle that hinders the Spirit of God from ruling in us, is our flesh. This is the last enemy that must be conquered. The one who walks in total victory is the one who understands the flesh, and has learned how to overcome it.

The Galatians failed terribly due to their ignorance of this truth. They attempted to perfect in the flesh what they had begun in the Spirit. (See Galatians 3:3). This made them fair game for those who desired to make a *showing in the flesh* that they might also *glory in the flesh,* (Galatians 6:12-13). They did not understand how absolutely corrupt the flesh really was, and they couldn't see that the power of sin in their flesh to fulfill its own lust and desires, also seeks to serve God in the perfection of the flesh itself. Because of this, the passions and desires of their flesh, their self-life, went unchecked, and they were compelled to do those things which they did not want to do. They didn't understand that if their flesh, or self-life, had any influence in serving God, it would also remain powerful to serve sin. The only way to conquer it from doing evil, was to first render it incapable of doing good, that is, good in the power of the flesh.

The letter to the Galatians was written to help them discover God's truth concerning the flesh, both in its service to sin, and to God. Paul desired to teach them that the Spirit, and the Spirit alone, is the only power of the Christian life. But it cannot have its full influence over the believer unless the flesh and its power is completely over-thrown. In revealing how this is to be accomplished, he then shares the key to God's revelation: ***the crucifixion and death of Jesus Christ is not only for the forgiveness of our sin, it is also the power that frees us from the roots and control of sin in our flesh-life.*** In the middle of his teaching about the walk of the Spirit, Paul says, *They that are Christ's have crucified the flesh with its passions and lust.* He is proclaiming the only way that total deliverance from the flesh can be obtained. The secret to *walking after the Spirit, and not the flesh,* is in not only in *understanding* the words, *crucify the flesh,* but to *experience* it as well.

In scripture, the term *the flesh* defines the entirety of our human nature under the power of sin, including our spirit, soul and body. After man's fall, God said, *Man is flesh,* (Genesis 6:3); all of the powers of his intellect, emotions, and will were now under total control of his flesh-life. Scripture speaks of the will of the flesh, the mind of the flesh, and the passions and lusts of the flesh, that in our flesh there is no good thing, and that the mind of the flesh is hostile towards God. There is nothing of the flesh that has any value in God's sight. Nothing! Nothing that comes out of the mind or will of the flesh, nothing that it thinks or does, regardless of the praise of man, means anything to God. Paul warns us that our greatest danger to walking with God is our confidence in the things of the flesh. Listening to its wisdom and following its leading is the cause of all our weakness and failure. In order to be truly pleasing to God, we must repent, or turn away from the flesh and its self-will and self effort, and turn to the work and the will of the Spirit of God in us. The only way to be made free from the power of the flesh is to have it removed, to have it crucified, and given over to death.

They that belong to Christ have crucified the flesh, (Galatians 5:24). We often speak of crucifying the flesh as something that must *be* done, but scripture always speaks of it as something that *has been* done. *Knowing this, that our old man was crucified with Him,* (Romans 6:6), *They that belong to Christ Jesus have crucified the flesh.* (Galatians 5:24). *The cross of our Lord Jesus Christ, through which the world has been crucified unto me, and I unto the world.* (Galatians 6:14 NASB). What Christ did on the cross, he did through the eternal Spirit for all mankind. All who come to him receive him as the crucified one, and obtain the merit of his death, and the power of his crucifixion. Each one who comes is united and identified with him, and is called to voluntarily know and remain in him. *They that are of Christ Jesus have - by virtue of their accepting the crucified Christ as their life - given up their flesh to the cross, which is the very essence of the person and character of Christ as he now lives in heaven; they have crucified the flesh with all its passions and lust.* (E.H. Hopkins, The Law of Liberty in the Spiritual Life.)

So what does it mean, *they have crucified the flesh?* Some are satisfied with the general truth that the cross takes away the curse of the flesh; others believe that they must cause the flesh suffering and pain in order to deny it and put it to death; while still others regard the moral influence that the thought of the cross will apply. There is an element of truth in each of these. But if they are to be experienced in power, we must go to this root thought: **to crucify the flesh means to give it over to the curse. The cross and the curse cannot be separated.** (See Deuteronomy 21:23; Galatians 3:13). To say, *Our old man has been crucified with him,* or, *I have been crucified with Christ,* means something both *severe* and *breathtaking.* This is what it means: *"I have 'seen' that my old nature, my self-life, deserves the curse and its penalty of death. I know there is no way around it except death on the cross. I voluntarily give myself over to death. I have accepted AS MY LIFE the Lord Jesus Christ, who came to give himself and his own flesh over to the cursed death of the cross, but who also received his new life by virtue of that same death on the cross. I give my old man, which is my flesh and my self-life, with its cursed and sinful will and ways, to the cross. It is firmly nailed there in Christ. I am dead to my flesh! I am free from my flesh! Each day in my union with Christ, I will keep my flesh there nailed to the cross of the Lord Jesus, and declare it dead through the power of the Holy Spirit."*

To unlock the power of this truth is dependent upon our knowing it, accepting it, and acting upon it. If I only know the cross in its substitution, but not in its fellowship, as Paul experienced, (Galatians 6:12), I will never fully encounter its power to sanctify me. As the truth of its fellowship is revealed, I can see that it is through faith alone that I enter and live in spiritual communion with Jesus. This is the only way to the throne of God. My spiritual union through faith becomes my moral union as well. I have the same mind, or moral disposition, as was in the Lord Jesus. I hate the flesh because it is sinful, only fit for the curse of God. And I accept the cross and its death to my flesh, secured for me through Jesus, as the only way that I will become free from the power of my self-life, and free to walk in this new life by the Spirit of Christ.

The way in which faith in the power of the cross acts both as the *revelation* and the *removal* of the curse, and the power of the flesh, is both simple, yet deep. I begin to understand that the greatest danger to my *living in the Spirit* is my yielding to the flesh, or my self-life, in all my attempts to follow God. This one thing will make the cross of Christ totally ineffective. (See 1 Corinthians 1:17; Galatians 3:3, 5:12-13; Philippians 3:3-4; Colossians 2:18-23). All that was of man and nature, of the law and human effort, was forever judged by God at the cross. There the flesh of man proved once and for all, with all of its great wisdom and religion, how much it hated and rejected the Son of God. There God proved that the only deliverance from the flesh was to give it over to death as something cursed. I must see the flesh as God does - to see that there is no good thing in it, and to accept the sentence of death that the cross brings to everything that is of the flesh in me. As I develop this habit in my soul, **I will learn to fear nothing in this world so much as myself.** I fear and tremble at the thought of allowing my flesh, my self-life, with my natural mind and will, to interfere with the Holy Spirit's work in me. My entire attitude towards Christ is in fear and trembling at the knowledge that my self-life is always lurking, even as an angel of light, to intrude itself into my new man, to deceive me into serving God through the power of my flesh, and not in the Spirit of Christ. But it is in this state of lonely fear, that I learn to believe completely that the Holy Spirit is my true need, and my true provision in filling up in me all that the flesh once possessed. This was the only way that Paul could say, *I have been crucified to the world.*

We often look for the reasons for so much failure in the Christian walk. And we think that because we understand something that the Galatians didn't grasp - that we are justified by faith alone - that we are not in the same danger that they were. Oh, how I pray we would know to what extent we have allowed the flesh, the self-life, to work in our Christian lives, as well! Let us pray and ask God for the grace to understand that it is our most bitter enemy in our life in Christ. Free grace does not only mean the pardon of sin, but it also means the power of the new life through the Holy Spirit to overcome the flesh and sin. Let's embrace what God says about the flesh, and all that comes with it, that it is sinful, condemned and cursed. Let us fear nothing so much as the lurking, secret power of our flesh and our self-life. Let's accept Paul's words, *In my flesh there dwells no good thing,* and, *The carnal mind is enmity against God.* If we are to be pleasing to God in all things, then let us ask him to give us the revelation that the Holy Spirit must possess our entire being - spirit, soul and body. Let us believe that as we daily yield our flesh and self-life to death on the cross, that Christ will accept our surrender, and by his power keep us in the life of the Spirit. And we will learn not only to *live in the Spirit,* free from the power of the flesh, but also to *walk in the Spirit* each day in all things.

PRAYER:

"Father, I ask you to reveal to me the full meaning of what your word says, that it is only as I have crucified the flesh, with its passions and lust, that I can walk in the Spirit.

"Lord, teach me to see that everything that is of my natural life and self is of the flesh, that the flesh has been tested by you, and found wanting, worthy of nothing but to be cursed and put to death. Convict me that in my flesh there is nothing good! Help me to turn my flesh over to the cross that it might be put to death.

"Oh God, give me your grace each day to fear you so that I will not allow my flesh to intrude into the work of the Holy Spirit in my life, that I would not grieve him. Teach me that it is the Holy Spirit who has been given to me to be the life of my life, that I no longer live by the flesh. And help me grasp with my whole being that it is now the power of the death and the life of our Lord Jesus Christ who lives in us.

"Lord Jesus, you sent the Holy Spirit to me, to secure for me the uninterrupted enjoyment of your presence and power within me. I give myself entirely over to you, that I would live completely under the leading of the Spirit. I desire with my

whole heart to regard my flesh as both cursed and crucified. And I solemnly and sincerely consent to live as a crucified one with you! Accept my full surrender, Oh Lord! I trust in you to keep me walking continuously in, and by, and through your Spirit. Amen."

CHAPTER 29

THE SPIRIT OF LOVE

But the fruit of the Spirit is love... Galatians 5:22

Now I beg you, brethren... through the love of the Spirit... Romans 15:30

Who also declared to us your love in the Spirit... Colossians 1:8

This chapter will lead us into the very center of the inner sanctuary of God. We are going to explore the love of the Spirit. It is not just one of the graces, or fruit of the Spirit - it is not even the principal of them - the Holy Spirit is nothing less than God's love itself coming to dwell in us. ***We have only as much of the Spirit in us as we have of love.***

God is *Spirit* - God is *Love*. These two words may define the character and nature of God more than any others found in scripture. As Spirit, he holds life within himself, he is independent of everything, and holds power over all things. Yet, he is able to penetrate and communicate himself to each of us as he desires. It is through the Spirit that God is the Father of spirits, the God of all creation, and the God and redeemer of mankind. Everything owes its life to the Spirit of God because God is love - love exists, and lives within him. We see this in the Father as he gave all his fullness to the Son, and we see it in the Son seeking all that he has in the Father. In this life of love between the Father in heaven, and the Son on the earth, the Spirit flowed between them as their bond of fellowship and union. The Father is the one who loves, a fountain of love - the Son is the loved one, the great reservoir of love, always receiving from the Father, and always returning that love. The Spirit is the living love that makes them one. In him dwells the divine life of love, which is always flowing. The same love that the Father loved the Son with now flows into us and seeks to fill us up as well. (See John 17:26). It is through the Spirit that the Father reveals and communicates to us his love. It was through the Spirit that Jesus was anointed and led to his work of love, preaching good news to the poor and deliverance to the captives. And through this same Spirit he loved us, even unto death on the cross. This same Spirit now comes to us filled with the fullness of the love of God the Father, and of the Lord Jesus Christ. The Spirit is the love of God.

The love of God has been poured out within our hearts through the Holy Spirit who was given to us, (Romans 5:5), is the first work of the Holy Spirit in us. What he gives is not only the faith, or the experience, of how much God loves us, but something even more - the love of God enters our hearts as a living power, and a spiritual reality. It cannot be otherwise, for the love of God is the reality of his existence, and the outpouring of the Spirit is the inpouring of love himself. The love of God himself takes over and possesses our hearts. It is the same love which the Father loved Jesus, and now all who are his. This love which is now poured out to all the world through the Spirit, is within us. If we know it and trust it, and give ourselves over to it - it is the very power to live in love. The Spirit is the life of the love of God, and the Spirit in us is the love of God residing within us.

Let's now consider the relationship between *our* spirit and love. If you will recall, man has a three-fold nature - spirit, soul and body - formed in creation, but ruined by the fall. The soul, as the center of our *self-consciousness*, was to be controlled by the spirit, which is the center of our *God-consciousness*. However, when the soul rebelled from the rule of the spirit, sin asserted itself, and pursued its satisfaction through the passions, desires and lust of the body. The fruit of that sin was that *self* sat on the throne of the soul and began to rule there, instead of God through our spirit. *Selfishness* emerged as the ruling power in man's life. The *self* that refused God his access to us through the spirit, also refused to see and recognize his fellowman. The horrible history of sin in the world is the story of the origin, growth, power and the reign of *SELF*. The life of *self,* or, *selfishness,* will only be conquered when the soul is completely submitted to the leadership and rule of the spirit, and *self* makes way for God. Only then will love flow into us from God, and back to him from us, and then out of us towards others. In other words, as our renewed spirit becomes the dwelling place of God's Spirit and his love, and as we yield ourselves to the Holy Spirit's complete control, the love of God will again become our life and joy. Jesus said to everyone who desired to be his disciple, *"Let him deny himself and follow me."* Many have tried to follow Jesus and his life of love, but they have failed because of this one thing - they did not deny themselves. *Self* following Jesus always fails - it cannot love as he loves.

If we understand this, then we are ready to live by the statement Jesus made, that the world will know that we are his disciples because we love. When the Holy Spirit truly changes us, and we are delivered from the power of sin and our self-life, the presence of God's love in us will be so real that it overflows from us as rivers of love. However, because so few today understand their spiritual calling to walk after the Spirit, there is little evidence that we are walking in love. We seem to flourish in anger, jealousy, offense, harsh judgments, unkind words and pride; we lack Christ's humility, patience and gentleness, and we are selfish, insensitive to the spiritual and social needs of those perishing and drowning all around us. We do not know the full extent that the Spirit is meant to be within us, because we have not accepted him for what the Lord Jesus intended him to be - we are more carnal than spiritual. We need to understand that to follow Christ means that we have the Spirit of Christ living in us. Only then are we changed into a fountain of love that springs up within us, and flows out of us in streams of living water. (See John 7:38-39).

This is how it was with the Corinthians. Paul said they were a church that was *in everything enriched in Christ, in all speech and knowledge... not lacking in any gifts.* (See 1 Corinthians 1:5-7). As a church they seemed to have everything, yet they lacked love. *For where there are envy, strife, and divisions among you, are you not carnal?* (1 Corinthians 3:3). Their examples of failure teaches us that we can be under the moving of the Holy Spirit, and be deeply affected in the soul - with its knowledge, speech, utterances, and faith - and yet our *self-life* is still not surrendered to him. Many gifts of the Spirit may be seen or manifested, but if the greatest gift of all is missing, we have failed. It is not enough for the Spirit to take hold of the natural characteristics of our soul and stir them to action for God. More is needed. The Spirit has entered the soul, that through it he may have total influence in both our spirit and soul. When the self-life has been surrendered and taken off the throne of our hearts, then God may rule and reign. And the evidence of this is love. Then we are free to live a life in the love of the Spirit.

The Galatian's church was not very different. Paul told them, *the fruit of the Spirit is love.* While their failure was not exactly the same as that of the Corinthians, they exhibited the same result - the Spirit's full control was not accepted in the inner life of love - and they failed. Their flesh ruled in them, as evidenced in much bitterness, envy and strife. (See Galatians 5:15-21). Even today throughout the Church, we see great trust in our giftings and knowledge, in the soundness of our doctrines, and the sincerity and importance of our ministries; but we still work hard with all of our plans, programs and promotions, taking great satisfaction in those things done in the strength of what is the uncrucified flesh. The Spirit is still not free to work out true holiness in us, or to release to us the life of the power of Christ's love. Let us pray that God would teach all of us who follow after Christ, that those who profess to *have* the Holy Spirit must prove it by manifesting Christ's love. The love of Christ in its gentleness in bearing wrong, and in its life of self-sacrifice to overcome wrong, must be repeated in the lives of those who are his. The Spirit is the love of God that has come down to us, and all who are under its wonderful power are saved.

The good news from the examples that the Corinthians and Galatians gave us is that the love of God has actually comes down to us - it is within our reach, and it dwells within us. From the first moment that we believed in Christ and were sealed with the Holy Spirit, God has been pouring out his love into our hearts. *The love of God has been poured out in our hearts by the Holy Spirit who was given to us,* (Romans 5:5). There may seem to be little evidence in our lives of this love of God, and we may have scarcely felt it or known it, but the truth is this - when the Holy Spirit came into our hearts, the love of God came with him. The two are inseparable! If we want to experience the presence of God's love, we must begin in simple faith in what God's word says. The Bible reveals the words that the Holy Spirit spoke for our benefit. If we receive his words in faith as truth, the Spirit will make it truth in us. Let us believe the promise of God that the Holy Spirit dwells within us, and as he possesses us, we are brought into the fullness of God's love. Because the dominion of our self-life has been so strong, the power of God's love and its outflow has been very weak. But if we believe that he dwells within us, and that he is the power of our life, then the love of God will be resident in our hearts.

If we believe that the Spirit of love is within us, then let us turn to the Father in prayer, and ask him to strengthen our hearts with his Spirit in our inner being, so that Christ may dwell in our hearts through faith, that we might be rooted and grounded in love, and that we would know this love in our experience, to the extent that we would be filled with all the fullness of God himself, which is his love. (See Ephesians 3:16-19). This is the same love that the Father loved the Lord Jesus with. Through the Holy

Spirit in us, this love then returns to its source as our love to God and Christ. And because the Spirit has revealed this love to all of God's children, our experience of it comes to us from God, and returning to him equals the love we have for one another. As water descends as the rain, and flows out as rivers or streams, and then rises again as vapor, so also is the love of God in its three forms - his love to us, our love to him, and our love for one another. If the Holy Spirit is in you, then the love of God dwells in you also. Let us believe this truth. Let's yield ourselves as a living sacrifice to his consuming fire, and what remains will be the purity of his love. Then we will know and understand, and prove that the Spirit of God is also the love of God.

PRAYER:

"Lord Jesus, I come to you as the divine expression of the Father's love. Your life on earth was a mission of love, and your death was its divine seal. Your one commandment was that we are to love; your one prayer to the Father was that we may be one, as you are one with the Father, and that his love would be in us. The primary reflection of your life and glory that you desire to see in us is that we would love as you love. You said that the world would know us by our love for one another. The Holy Spirit that you have sent to us is the same Spirit that lived in you, as you sacrificed for love, teaching us to live and die for others, as you did.

"Lord Jesus, I pray that your Church and your people would learn to love as you love. Please deliver us from every-thing within us that is still selfish and unloving. Teach us to yield up our entire self-life, which is unable to love, to the cross. Teach us in our spirits that we are able to love, because the Holy Spirit, the Spirit of love, lives in us. And teach us, Oh Lord, to love in our actions and service, to sacrifice our self and live for others, so that love may understand its power, and that it may increase and be perfected .

"Finally, Lord Jesus, help us to believe that because you live in us, your love lives in us too, and that we can demonstrate love just as you do. You are the very love of God! We believe in the love of God - help us Lord Jesus in our unbelief! May your own Spirit break through and fill up our whole spirit, soul and body with your love. Amen!"

CHAPTER 30

THE UNITY OF THE SPIRIT

That you walk... with all lowliness and gentleness, with long suffering, bearing with one another in love, endeavoring to keep the unity of the Spirit in the bond of peace. There is one body and one Spirit. Ephesians 4:1-4

There are diversities of gifts, but the same Spirit... But one and the same Spirit works all these things, distributing to each individually as He wills. For by one Spirit we were all baptized into one body - and have all been made to drink into one Spirit. 1 Corinthians 12:4, 11, 13

In the first three chapters of the book of Ephesians, Paul establishes the glory of God in Christ as the head of the Church, and the Church as his body, inhabited by the Holy Spirit, destined to be filled with all the fullness of God, (see Ephesians 1:23). Having been lifted up into heaven, (Ephesians 2:6), with his life now hidden in Christ in God, (Colossians 3:3), the believer now comes back down, in union with Christ, to his life in the earth. The first lesson Paul gives regarding this new life and walk on the earth (see Ephesians 4:1-4), is that through the Spirit we are united with Christ in heaven, *and* with his body on the earth. The Spirit dwells *in Christ, in us, and in all of his body.* The fullness of Christ in the Holy Spirit will only be found where there is unity in relationship between the individual believer and the body of Christ. When the concerns of the body are for the unity of the Spirit to remain intact among us, the primary character trait exhibited will be humility. Only as we prefer others more than ourselves, sacrificing for one another in love, even where there are great differences and shortcomings, will we fulfill the new commandment to love one another. And the Spirit of Christ, who is the Spirit of Love sacrificing itself wholly for others, will be revealed to the world.

We desperately need this teaching today. As we saw in the previous chapter, Paul admonished the Corinthians, who operated abundantly in the manifestations of the gifts of the Spirit, but who lacked the grace and fruit of the Spirit. They did not understand that there were many members, and many different gifts within the body, but there was only one Spirit, and all of them were baptized into him, and were only members of one body. They had not encountered the more excellent way, the best of gifts, which was the love that does not seek its own, but only finds its fulfillment in others.

To the believer who would yield to the leading of the Holy Spirit, and to the Church, the body of Christ, as it longs to experience the power of God: embrace the unity of the Spirit as truth, a rich spiritual blessing. Pastor Otto Stockmaier said, *Have a deep reverence for the work of the Holy Spirit within you.* That encouragement needs to include, *Have a deep reverence for the work of the Holy Spirit in your brother or sister in Christ, as well.* This is not easy, and even mature believers often fail here. The reasons should be obvious. As children we are taught to observe the differences between things and one another - in a sense, to discriminate. Conversely, cooperation - or harmonizing in the midst of diversity - is a much higher lesson that usually comes much later. That lesson finds its most striking examples among believers and the Church. It does not take a lot for us to see where we differ from one another in our doctrines, movements, and viewpoints. But true grace saves a place for the unity of the Spirit, and maintains faith in the power of God's love to preserve our living union with one another, in spite of our differences.

God's command to each believer is to keep the unity of the Spirit. It fulfills the new commandment to love one another in a new way, tracing its love back to the Spirit in which it has life. To obey this, we must be careful that it is the unity of the Spirit we seek, not the unity of the flesh. There is a big difference. There is unity among us that is based on our movements and denominations, our churches or preferences, our customs or creeds, and even our Christian nationalities, but these are all more of the flesh than of the Spirit.

It is only as we seek to know the Spirit within us that we are able to find his power to connect and unite with others. There is an ability, or power in each of us that can foster an earthly unity, that is totally of the flesh; it will hinder the true unity of the Spirit. We must recognize that within our natural life - the flesh - there is no power to love or be united; everything in us is selfish and does not seek the true unity of the Spirit. Only as we humble ourselves and believe that it is from God alone in us, can we ever possibly be united with what is displeasing or offensive. Let us be thankful that he is in us; he is able to do what we cannot do - conquer our self-life, and love *through us* to those who seem so unloveable.

Seek to know and value what is in the brother or sister you are united with. If it is in you, it is also in them - a beginning, a hidden seed containing the divine life. They are, like you, still surrounded by much that is of their flesh, and they're often very trying and difficult. We need a heart that is humbled by how unworthy we are - a heart ready to love and quick to forgive. This is what Jesus did on his last night - *"The spirit is indeed willing, but the flesh is weak."* We need to look at what is in our brother or sister that reflects the image and likeness of God. Do not judge them by what they have within themselves, but by what they are in Christ. The same Spirit which, by God's grace, gives life to you, is also living in them. As you acknowledge this, the unity of the Spirit will triumph over your prejudices and dislikes, and the Spirit in you will bind you to your brother or sister in the unity of a life that comes only from God.

We must maintain the unity of the Spirit in active fellowship with one another. The parts of our individual bodies are all connected together, and maintained through the life in our blood. *In the Spirit we are all baptized into one body.* There is one body of Christ, and there is one Spirit of Christ. The inner union of life within each individual part of Christ's body must be strengthened, and find its true expression in the manifested communion of love to the rest of his body. Cultivate fellowship with others, even with those you may have differences with, so that the unity is not more from the flesh than the Spirit. In all your thoughts and judgements, seek to exercise the love that thinks no evil of other believers. Never say an unkind word about another child of God, or anyone, for that matter. Love every believer, regardless if they agree with you, or are pleasing to you. Love them for the sake of the Spirit of God which is also in them. Pursue love for all of God's children within your reach, including those who may still be immature, who may not have the Spirit living in them, or are grieving him. The work of the Holy Spirit is to build us up and prepare us as a dwelling place for God. Yield yourself to the Spirit so that he can do his work. Then recognize that he is doing the same work in your brother or sister, and that you need each other in the fellowship of the Spirit to fully complete the work he started, so that you can grow together with one another in the unity of love.

In the true unity of the Church, there is a worldwide intercession that rises up to God through Christ Jesus, "*That they may be one as we are one.*" (John 17:22). The Church is one in the life of Christ and the love of the Spirit. But it is not yet one in the manifest unity of the Spirit. Therefore we must continue to obey his command, *keep the unity.* Intercede with Christ for the powerful outpouring of the Holy Spirit upon all nations, churches, and groups of believers. When the tide is low, each small pool along the shore becomes separated from others by a rocky barrier. But as the tide rises, the barriers are flooded over, and the pools and their inhabitants all meet again in one great ocean. So it is with the Church of Jesus Christ. As the Spirit floods each of our dry grounds, and as he is known and honored in us, our individual self lives will disappear, and we will know the power of the Spirit of Unity in ourselves and in others.

When will this prayer be fulfilled, "*That they may all be one, that the world may know that You have sent Me, and have loved them as You have loved Me."*? Let us each resolve that the one mark of our lives, the proof that we are sons of God, is that we have and know the indwelling Holy Spirit. This requires that we each give ourselves up entirely to his life, his way of thinking and acting. He must have full control of each of us. And we must abide daily in the conscious understanding that he dwells in us. We need to pray continuously that the Father may give us, according to his riches in glory, strength and might in our inner man. It is in the faith of the three-in-one God - the Father giving us the Spirit in the name of the Son, and the Spirit dwelling in us, in direct contact with the Father and the Son - that the Holy Spirit will take full possession of us throughout our entire being. The more he has of us, and works within us, the more spiritual our life becomes, and the more our self-life slips away, allowing the Spirit of Christ to use us in the building up, and the knitting together of believers into a holy habitation of God. The Spirit of Christ in us will be an anointing oil, the oil of consecration, setting us apart and equipping us to be his messengers of the Father's love. In the humility and meekness that comes in abiding in Christ, we will set aside our differences within his body. The Holy Spirit will demonstrate that he belongs to all who believe, as much as to us. And through us his love will expand to all around, to teach, edify and bless.

PRAYER:

"Lord Jesus, as you prayed, "Holy Father, keep them one as we are one," your one great desire was that they, and we, who follow you, would be united in the Spirit of unity and love. We

who believe today, continue to cry out to you to keep us, that we might be one! Please pray for us that we may be perfected as one so that the world may know that the Father loves us as he loved you. Thank you for stirring believers everywhere to be united with one another that the manifestation of the body of Christ to the world would be that your people love one another and are united to each other.

"We pray that every believer may know that the Spirit who lives in him or her, also lives in their brother or sister. May we all walk in the love and humility of the unity of the Spirit with all whom we come in contact. May your leaders in the Church understand that the unity of the Spirit is more important than all the human bonds of union, or movements, or thoughts. We pray that all who have clothed themselves with Christ, above all things, clothed themselves with love, the bond of righteousness, and peace.

"Finally, Lord Jesus, we pray that you would unite your people in prayer so that we would all be filled with the Holy Spirit, and that your presence would be manifest to us all. Then we shall be truly one - one Spirit and one body! Amen."

CHAPTER 31

FILLED WITH THE SPIRIT

Be filled with the Spirit, speaking to one another... Ephesians 5:18-19

These words are not a suggestion, but a command. And it is a command that stems from the promise of the Father, that we can claim for ourselves - *we are to be filled with the Holy Spirit.* I am convinced that this should be the natural and sustained experience of every sincere believer in Christ. It is also the only way that we are able to sustain this new life in Christ - abiding in him, keeping his commands, and bearing much fruit. Yet so many hold this *command* in small regard, and dismiss the idea that it is possible, or even reasonable, that we should be expected to keep it!

The reason for this may be due to our misunderstanding of the words of the command. On the day of Pentecost, and on later occasions, being filled with the Spirit was usually accompanied by supernatural manifestations of joy, power, and great excitement. However, these may seem somewhat inconsistent with the daily experiences of ordinary life. Because of the miraculous nature and experiences associated with being filled with the Spirit, many believed it was only something for special people, or special occasions. Many believers have felt this was not something they could ever hope for, or if received, could possibly maintain.

The message I bring to you is that the command - *Be filled with the Spirit* - is for *every* believer, that the promise and the power has been given for all. May God awaken within our hearts the desire for this to be true in each of us, and give us the confidence that this promise of his is meant for us, and it will become our very own.

In my country of South Africa, where we often suffer from drought, there are two types of dams, or reservoirs, that we use to capture and store water. On some farms there are flowing springs, but the stream coming forth is too weak to use for irrigation, so a reservoir is built to collect the water. The result is that the gentle and quiet flowing stream trickles and pours into the reservoir each day and night. Then there are other farms that have no springs, so the reservoir is built in a dry stream bed or hollow. Following a heavy rain, which is often accompanied by a violent and rushing torrent of water, these reservoirs may be completely filled within a few hours. However, the quiet trickling stream of the first farm is the more reliable way. Even though it is apparently weaker, it remains permanent. In those places where water and rainfall is uncertain, their dry reservoirs may be empty for months at a time.

The two kinds of reservoirs represent the two ways that the Holy Spirit can come into us. There are times when there is an outpouring of the Spirit for revival, or great salvations in a new land, as on the day of Pentecost, where people are suddenly and powerfully filled with the Holy Spirit. In those moments of sudden revival and salvation, great enthusiasm and joy is evident all around, found in the presence and the power of the Spirit. And yet there are potential pitfalls for those who receive the Spirit this way. These sudden and torrential encounters are often too dependent upon others, or they extend only to the most easily reached areas of the soul's superficial life; they are unable to penetrate the depths of the will and the inner life. Yet, there are other believers who have never experienced any sudden or explosive encounters, yet the fullness of the Spirit is seen in them by their deep and intense devotion to Jesus Christ. They walk in his light and the consciousness of his presence, in simple trust and obedience, and in love and humility. They are like Barnabas, *a son of consolation, a good man, and full of the Holy Spirit.*

Which of these is the better way of being filled with the Spirit? The answer is easy - both! There are areas in South Africa on which both of the previously mentioned reservoirs are to be found right next to each other. There are even some farms where they use both means. The regular, quiet trickling spring-fed stream keeps them supplied year-round, even in times of drought, yet they are ready to receive and store up large quantities of water during the heavy rains. Likewise there are believers in whom the springs rise up within, and quietly stream forth, filling them up daily. And there are others who are only content with the mighty encounters of the Spirit, coming like a mighty rushing wind, or a torrential rainfall, or the baptism of fire. We would be wise and blessed if we recognize God in both, always ready to be filled up fresh in whichever way he comes.

What are the conditions to be filled with the Spirit? According to the word of God, there is only one - faith! It is only through faith that we can see and receive the invisible - that we can see and receive God himself. The cleansing from sin and the surrender to God in obedience, which were the conditions of the first reception of the Spirit, (see John 20:22), are the fruit of the faith that recognized what sin, the blood of Jesus, and the love and the will of the Father are. I am not speaking of that experience here. I'm addressing those believers who have been faithful to obey, but still have not received the complete filling up by the Spirit that they long for. They must discover what is remaining in them that still needs to be set aside, or removed. All filling up requires first an emptying out. I'm not speaking here of the cleansing of sin and the surrender of our will unto full obedience. That is always the first step. I'm speaking now to those who believe they have already met all of God's requirements, and yet are still waiting for his complete infilling. Please remember that the first condition of all filling is to be *empty*. A reservoir is nothing more than a great hollow, or emptiness, which is prepared and waiting for the water to be poured into it. All true abiding for the fullness of the Spirit is always preceded by emptying ourselves. "*I sought the blessing long and earnestly,*" said one, "*and I wondered why it did not come. At last I found it was because there was no room in my heart to receive it.*"

There are several things to consider in the emptying of ourselves:

- A deep dissatisfaction with our life in Christ as we have had it until now,
- A deep understanding of how much of it has been in our own wisdom and the work of the flesh,
- The discovery, confession, and giving up of everything in our life that we have tried to control, that our self-life has ruled over, of everything that we have not submitted to the Lord Jesus,
- A deep conviction of our inability and complete helplessness to even understand or claim what is being offered to us,
- A surrender in the poverty of our spirit, to wait upon the Lord in his great mercy and power, *according to his riches in glory to strengthen us mightily by His Spirit in the inner man,*
- Waiting for the Lord - longing, thirsting, crying, pleading, praying without ceasing for the Father to fulfill his promise to us, and to take full possession of us within.

This is the kind of emptying that is needed in order to be filled.

In addition to being emptied, we need *faith* which can accept, receive, and maintain the gift. It is through faith in Christ, and the Father, that the divine fullness will flow into us. It was to the Ephesians that Paul said, *Be filled with the Spirit,* that he also said, *In Christ, having believed, you were sealed with the Holy Spirit of promise,* (see Ephesians 1:13). He was referring to what they had already received. The spring was within them, but it had to be opened up and a place (reservoir) made for it that it would flow into, and fill their inner being. This is not by their power - Jesus had said, *"He that believes in Me, rivers of living water will flow out of him,"* (John 7:38). The fullness of the Spirit is only in Christ, and our receiving it comes only through our unbroken life-union with him. The never ending flow of the life-sap from Jesus, the living vine, must be met by our simple, yet ceaseless faith that the flowing of the spring within us is a result of our complete dependance on him. It is by the faith *of* Jesus, not our faith, that the inflow will grow ever stronger until it becomes an overflow.

And there is more. We may have faith in Jesus to be filled with the Spirit, but not the faith for the Father's special gift, or the prayer for his greater fullness. To the Ephesians, who had the Spirit within them as a down payment for their eternal inheritance, Paul prayed to the Father, *that He would grant you, according to the riches of His glory, that you may be strengthened with power through His Spirit in the inner man,* (Ephesians 3:16). The verbs both imply an action, something done at once. The expression, *according to the riches of His glory,* indicates a great exhibition of his love and power, something very special and from God. They already had the Spirit within them, but Paul prayed that the Father would intervene and give them such a sense of the presence and the fullness of the Holy Spirit, that the indwelling life of Christ - his love which surpasses all knowledge and understanding - would be known and experienced by them, to the extent that they would be filled with all the fullness of God himself. At the time of the great flood of Noah, the windows of heaven, and the fountains of the deep were both opened at the same time. It is the same in the fulfilling of the promise of the Spirit, *I will pour floods upon the dry ground.* The deeper our faith in the reality of the indwelling Spirit, and the simpler our waiting on him, the more abundantly will be the outpouring of the Spirit from the heart of the Father into our hearts.

It is only by faith! God loves to appear to us in a lowly and unlikely form, clothing himself with humility, which he also wants us to wear. *The kingdom of heaven is like a seed...* only faith can recognize the glory that is in it. This was the way of the Son of God on the earth - this is the way of the Spirit of God in the heart. He asks us to believe when there is nothing to see. By faith we believe that the fountain that springs up and flows forth is within us, even when it seems to be completely dried up. Take the time to go into the inner places of your heart, and give praise and thanksgiving unto God, and worship him with the faith and assurance of Jesus, that the fountain of the Holy Spirit is within you. Realize his presence, and remain in it; let the Spirit himself fill your spirit with this heavenly truth - he dwells in you. He is not limited to your thoughts or feelings, but deeper still in the life of your life, beyond what you can see or feel, he is there in his temple, his hidden dwelling place. When faith trusts that it has what it has asked for, it becomes patient, and rejoices in thanksgiving, where before the flesh would murmur and complain. It trusts in the unseen Jesus, and the hidden Spirit. It believes in the power of the little seed, and gives glory to him who is able to do exceedingly and abundantly above and beyond all that he can ask or think, or even imagine. (See Ephesians 3:20-21). Do not expect for the fullness of the Spirit to come in the way of your natural understanding; expect him to come as Christ came into the world, without form or beauty, and in ways that might seem foolish to your flesh or human understanding. Expect his divine power to be revealed in the middle of your great weakness. Humble yourself before him, and you will receive his divine wisdom. Be willing to become nothing, because God chooses *the things which are not to bring to nothing the things that are,* (1 Corinthians 1:28). You will learn that you are not to glory in your flesh, but to glory in the Lord. In the deep joy that comes from a life lived out in daily obedience, and the simplicity of the faith of Christ, you shall know what it is to be filled with the Spirit.

PRAYER:

"Father, the fullness of your love is like an endless ocean, beyond our ability to see or comprehend. We thank you that in the revelation of your Son, it pleased you that all of the fullness of Deity is in Christ, and that we have fullness in our human

life in him. I thank you that his Church on the earth, in spite of its weakness, is his body, the fullness of him who fills all things. We thank you that in him we are made full, and that by the powerful working of your spirit in us, and the indwelling presence of the Lord Jesus, and in the deep knowledge of your great love, we may be filled with all the fullness of God.

"Oh God, we thank you that the Holy Spirit is the bearer to us of all the fullness of Christ, and that as we are filled with the Spirit we are also made full of his fullness. We thank you that countless believers before us have been baptized and filled with the Holy Spirit. Oh Lord, make us full! Make me full! I pray for all the saints everywhere that they may be filled with all the fullness of God. May the Holy Spirit take me and keep possession of my deepest innermost life. Let it overflow from me into the world around me, where you have me. I dedicate my body as the temple of your Holy Spirit, filled with your divine life. I believe, by faith, that you hear and honor this prayer.

"Oh Lord Jesus, I pray that your church is filled with the Holy Spirit, Oh Lord Jesus, I pray that I am filled with the Holy Spirit. Thank you! Amen"

THE END OF THIS BOOK,
AND THE BEGINNING OF YOUR
TRUE LIFE IN CHRIST.

Made in the USA
Monee, IL
03 July 2023